CHRISTIAN ENCOUNTERS

WINSTON CHURCHILL

CHRISTIAN ENCOUNTERS

WINSTON CHURCHILL

JOHN PERRY

THOMAS NELSON
Since 1798

NASHVILLE   DALLAS   MEXICO CITY   RIO DE JANEIRO

Published in Nashville, Tennessee. Thomas Nelson is a trademark of Thomas
Nelson, Inc.

Published in association with the literary agency of Wolgemuth & Associates, Inc.

Thomas Nelson, Inc., titles may be purchased in bulk for educational, business,
fund-raising, or sales promotional use. For information, please e-mail
SpecialMarkets@ThomasNelson.com.

Library of Congress Cataloging-in-Publication Data

Perry, John, 1952–
  Winston Churchill / by John Perry.
    p. cm. — (Christian encounters)
  Includes bibliographical references.
  ISBN 978-1-59555-306-5
  1. Churchill, Winston, 1874-1965. 2. Prime ministers—Great Britain—
Biography. 3. Great Britain—Politics and government—1936-1945. 4. Great
Britain—Politics and government—1945-1964. I. Title.
  DA566.9.C5P44 2010
  941.084092—dc22
  [B]
                                    2009050624

Printed in the United States of America

10 11 12 13 14 HCI 6 5 4 3 2 1

This book is dedicated to my son,

CHARLES THOMAS PERRY,

who shares a keen appreciation

for history with me, and with the grandfather

he never knew, whom, as his father,

I expected to teach about unconditional love,

but who taught me instead.

CONTENTS

FIRST LESSONS

To his mother's great surprise, Winston Leonard Spencer-Churchill was born on November 30, 1874, in the middle of a party. Jennie Jerome Churchill had been enjoying the St. Andrew's Day ball after a day of shooting at Blenheim, her father-in-law's monumental estate in Oxfordshire, two hours by train from London. Along with the other ladies up for the weekend, she had followed the men on the hunt that morning, then taken a bumpy ride in a pony cart. Once the contractions began, the process advanced so fast she couldn't make it upstairs to her room. Her child was born in a long-vacant bedroom on the first floor serving as a cloakroom for the evening. Originally it had been part of the household chaplain's apartment, though later generations considered it inconvenient and uncomfortable. There were no baby clothes in the house, so the newborn wore an infant's tiny white nightshirt borrowed from a neighbor in the nearby village of Woodstock.

Announcing the news in a letter to Jennie's mother, her husband wrote that the birth was caused by a fall.

Jennie had been married only seven months when Winston arrived. He could have been premature, yet seemed by all accounts to be a full-term baby. This would explain why his parents' wedding had not been the great society affair typical of the British aristocracy. Jennie was a Brooklyn-born American whose wealthy father, Leonard Jerome, had made and lost several fortunes in stocks, real estate, and trade. He named his middle daughter in honor of the famous soprano Jenny Lind, who was likely his mistress at the time his daughter was born. The Jeromes lived in Italy when Jennie was a girl, and her mother, Clara, loved European society. Mrs. Jerome was a take-charge, self-confident kind of woman whose ancestors included an officer in George Washington's army and a great-grandmother who was full-blooded Iroquois. After two years in Trieste, New York seemed boring and unfashionable, prompting Clara to move with her three marriageable daughters to Paris in search of adventure, culture, and titled husbands.

In the summer of 1873, when Jennie was nineteen, her mother rented a villa for the season on the Isle of Wight off the southern coast of England. During their stay they were invited to a party aboard the Prince of Wales's yacht, the HMS *Ariadne*. Lord Randolph Henry Spencer-Churchill, second surviving son of the seventh duke of Marlborough and a friend of his royal highness, was also aboard, and Jennie met him that afternoon. Three days later they were engaged.

Neither family got what they expected from the match. The duke saw the Jeromes as crass, self-made American tradesmen; the second son of an English duke was a notch below the French prince or count Clara was trolling for on Jennie's behalf. Even so, each side had something the other badly wanted. Marlborough craved some of that crass American money to shore up his badly depleted finances and maintain his gargantuan estate. And Clara allowed that becoming Lady Randolph Churchill might be a suitable goal for her daughter Jennie after all.

In the end, the Jerome family snagged their noble pedigree, and the duke received a handsome settlement from his new American relatives. Like many old noble families in Britain, the dukes of Marlborough were rich in property and poor in cash. The duke's income from his various estates historically amounted to £40,000 a year, roughly equivalent to $6 million today. This, it turned out, was scarcely enough to keep the lamps lit: some dukes had incomes four or five times as high. For months the Jeromes and Spencer-Churchills haggled over the dowry, with Leonard Jerome finally agreeing to a marriage settlement of £50,000, about $7.5 million in modern dollars, on which Lord Randolph would draw £3,000 per year in interest. The duke added an allowance of £1,200 on top of that.

By tradition the duke's second son should have been wed with all the pomp and panoply Blenheim could muster, a celebration marking one of the highlights of the London social calendar. Instead, Randolph and Jennie were married quietly at the British embassy in Paris on April 15, 1874. The duke and duchess were conspicuously absent. Though the Prince of Wales sent his secretary as his personal representative, the event was so low-key, there wasn't even a wedding announcement in the London *Times*. The duke and Jerome both seemed eager to hush up the news rather than crow with fatherly pride. At least there was a big welcome-home party for Lord Randolph and his bride at Blenheim, including the traditional honor of estate workers unhitching the carriage horses at the train station and pulling the couple home in the traces themselves.

Winston Churchill's birthplace was (and remains) one of the largest and most opulent private homes ever built. Blenheim had been conceived as a gift from a grateful nation to the first duke of Marlborough, John, and his wife, Sarah, for the duke's victory over the French during the War of the Spanish Succession in 1704. The king of Spain had died without an heir, and various European powers, including England and France, were jockeying to take advantage of the situation. Marlborough defeated the armies of Louis XIV in the Battle of Blenheim, which gave its name to the palatial home.

The house was unfinished and hopelessly over budget when the duke and duchess fell out of favor with their benefactor, Queen Anne, and all work on the project ground to a halt. Later, King George I helped them finish construction. By the time all was completed, the house had cost the modern equivalent of $100 million, not counting the many bills that were never paid.

Succeeding generations of dukes found the house ill suited for daily living and ruinously expensive to maintain. The kitchen and dining room were on separate floors; the lead roof covered three acres; the painters counted a thousand windows; the library was 180 feet long, or about two NBA basketball courts end to end.

Over the generations the house changed along with succeeding dukes' interest in art, architecture, spiritual matters, gardening, hunting, politics, and various aspects of family life. John, the first duke, commissioned magnificent tapestries illustrating his famous battlefield victories. Later dukes added great paintings, libraries, sculpture, and other treasures to the house and grounds. John also employed a personal chaplain (whose apartment his ninth-generation grandson Winston would be born in) and tempered his military outlook with a genuine sense of piety. His wife, Sarah, had a different view of religion, declaring that the church was "a spell to enchant weak minds."[1]

Winston's grandfather, John Winston Spencer-Churchill, the seventh duke, had a religious viewpoint that picked up where the first duke left off, though none of it seems to have rubbed off on his son Randolph, Winston's father. Inheriting the dukedom in 1860, he declared, "I cannot be grateful enough to God for all the goodness He has shown me. My position here is really, of its kind, quite perfect, and if only I keep well I am thoroughly satisfied."

The seventh duke seems to have been pious in the extreme. His first bill in the House of Lords after taking his ancestral seat was to observe the Sabbath by forbidding military bands to play in parks on Sundays. And he shared the disapproving Victorian view of any art from earlier times that displayed voluptuous, sensual nudes, regardless of its quality or value. He ordered nine Titians and a Rubens removed from his walls and locked in a room above the bakery. When the bakery caught fire in 1861, the paintings were destroyed. The next day at morning prayers the family sang, "God moves in mysterious ways His wonders to perform."[2]

Blenheim was a historic, grand, influential little world safely enfolded in the arms of the mighty British Empire. Great Britain was the most powerful nation in history, eventually commanding one-fourth of the world's population and almost a third of its land mass. For nearly three hundred years since defeating the Spanish Armada in 1588, Britain had been the unchallenged ruler of the oceans as well. In the imperial balance, the British demanded raw materials and cheap labor from their far-flung colonies in return for the blessings of civilization: roads, railways, schools, hospitals, Western-style government (whether they wanted it or not), and the Christian religion (ditto).

It was, in fact, a culture awash in the trappings of Protestant Christianity. At her coronation thirty-seven years before Winston was born, Queen Victoria swore the monarchs' ancient oath to uphold the Anglican Church. Winston's father and every other member of Parliament recited an oath of loyalty in the name of God before they took office. Yet for all its part in the fabric of public life in Victorian England, religion meant little to most people. It was so commonplace as to be invisible. As it has through so much of history, a mask of religious conformity and moral propriety hid people's true thoughts and actions.

It was thanks to a slip of that mask that Winston's earliest childhood memories were not of Blenheim or his parents' home in London, but of Ireland. Winston's uncle Charles, Marquess of Blandford and heir to the dukedom, was a notorious womanizer who had a liaison with the Countess of Aylesford. The countess was also a mistress of the Prince of Wales, whose long list of affairs was an open secret. When the countess became pregnant, the prince wanted the marquess to divorce his wife and marry the countess to relieve him from any implied responsibility. The marquess refused, and Lord Randolph, trying to help his brother, foolishly went to the Princess of Wales threatening to publish her husband's letters to the countess. He warned that if he did, her husband "would never sit upon the throne of England," adding, "I have the crown of England in my pocket."[3]

When the prince, oldest son of Queen Victoria and later King Edward VII, learned what Lord Randolph had done, he challenged him to a duel. Randolph refused to risk killing the heir apparent and offered an apology instead. The prince accepted, but the doors of high society slammed shut on Randolph and Jennie; they became instant social outcasts. Victoria's prime minister, Benjamin Disraeli, came up with a face-saving solution that would get Randolph out of the public eye long enough for tempers to cool. He appointed the Duke of Marlborough Lord Lieutenant of Ireland, the king's viceroy, with Randolph going along as his private secretary. And so young Winston, who by then had already sailed the Atlantic to meet his American relatives, moved to Dublin a month after his second birthday.

Since 1801 Catholic Ireland had been an unwilling member of the Protestant United Kingdom. By the time Lord Randolph took up his duties in Dublin, a movement by Catholics promoting Irish autonomy was well established and sometimes violent. Years later Churchill remembered walks outside the viceregal lodge in Phoenix Park and seeing men his nurse told him were members of Sinn Fein, which she considered a dangerous pro-independence, anti-British mob of hooligans. A friend they met in the park one afternoon was murdered days later, possibly by the same people. In the nurse's mind there was no doubt those young thugs were murderers.

Ireland's history was peppered with religion-inspired violence. Young Winston went to visit Emo Park, seat of Lord

Portarlington, who, Churchill later wrote, "was explained to me as a sort of uncle. Of this place I can give a very clear description, though I have never been there since I was four or four and a half. The central point in my memory is a tall white stone tower which we reached after a considerable drive. I was told it had been blown up by Oliver Cromwell. I understood definitely that he had blown up all sorts of things and was therefore a very great man."[4]

Typical of the Victorian upper-class attitude about children, Lord and Lady Randolph spent almost no time with Winston or his little brother, John Strange Spencer-Churchill, born in 1880 in Dublin. Randolph busied himself with his duties and his politics while Jennie moved in the British social circles and became renowned for her grace and skill at fox hunting. Winston's first memory of his mother was "in Ireland in a riding habit, fitting like a skin and often beautifully spotted with mud. . . . My mother seemed to me like a fairy princess: a radiant being possessed of limitless riches and power. She shone for me like the Evening Star. I loved her dearly—but at a distance."

It was Elizabeth Everest, the boys' nurse, who took care of them day and night and gave them the love, affection, attention, affirmation, and instruction they needed and that no one else was there to give. Trying to say "woman," Winston christened her "Woomy," and addressed her and wrote to her as "Oom," "Woom," or "Woomany" for the rest of her life. Woomany fed the boys their meals, took them on their walks, and held them when they cried. Woomy was with Winston when he was tossed from a donkey in Dublin and got a concussion.

Early on in their lives she gave the boys generous doses of

her own religious viewpoint, which was Low Church (simple in practice as opposed to the pageantry of official Anglicanism) and anti-Catholic. Winston remembered her being "nervous about the Fenians" in Ireland. "I gathered these were wicked people and there was no end to what they would do if they had their way."

Woomany also taught Winston his first lessons, until Lady Randolph felt it was time to begin a more formal education and hired a nursery tutor named Miss Hutchinson when Winston was five or six. While he had loved learning by doing and exploring with Woomany, something approaching real schoolwork was a bore. The tutor started teaching Winston reading and arithmetic, an irritation that prompted him to hide outside in the shrubs when it was time for class. Preshadowing both his trouble in school and his natural inclination to command, he rang for the maid after one especially dreary session. When the servant arrived he instructed her, "Take away Miss Hutchinson. She is very cross."[5]

The duke and Lord Randolph returned to England in 1880, Randolph to immerse himself in national politics and, along with his wife, gradually rejoin the social set his conflict with the Prince of Wales had closed off to them four years before. Lord and Lady Randolph settled into a fashionable house in London, constantly on the go, entertaining frequently, and making up for lost time during their Irish exile. Under Woomany's care, their sons divided their time between London, Blenheim, and summer trips to Mrs. Everest's relatives on the Isle of Wight. Her brother-in-law, John Balaam, took Winston on long walks and told him stories about shipwrecks and the Zulu wars in Africa. At Blenheim there was always riding and games, along with swimming and boating in the lake.

This idyllic life ended abruptly when his parents decided to send him away to boarding school, the standard for educating older boys from wealthy families while the girls continued with tutors at home. Winston dreaded the idea of leaving the comfort and familiar surroundings of the nursery for an unknown place filled with strangers. His mother took him to St. George's School in Ascot, one of the most fashionable and expensive schools in the country, and stayed for tea with the headmaster before she left. Winston was, he later recalled, "miserable at the idea of being left alone among all these strangers in this great, fierce, formidable place. After all I was only seven, and I had been so happy in my nursery with all my toys. I had such wonderful toys: a real steam engine, a magic lantern [an early form of slide projector], and a collection of soldiers already nearly a thousand strong. Now it was to be all lessons."[6]

The next two years were among the most miserable of Winston's life. The headmaster at St. George's, Herbert Sneyd-Kynnersley, was a high Anglican, anti-Catholic archconservative who has gone down in history as a wild-eyed sadist. Though at least one of Winston's classmates considered the headmaster "the only real positive influence" on Winston during his years there, and another student decided Kynnersley was "stupid rather than sadistic," Churchill's recollection in *My Early Life*, an autobiography published in 1930, leaves an indelible mental image. The headmaster's floggings, with a birch rod, typically consisted of twenty strokes on a boy's bare bottom, though by the third blow or so the rod was drawing blood. The beatings were, Churchill believed, more severe than anything that would be tolerated in a state reformatory.

As he described the scene: "Two or three times a month the whole school was marshalled in the Library, and one or more delinquents were hauled off to an adjoining apartment by two head boys, and there flogged until they bled freely, while the rest sat quaking, listening to their screams."

During this impressionable period Winston was also formulating his views of organized religion. His parents didn't go to church or practice whatever faith they had at home. What he picked up so far was from godly and compassionate Mrs. Everest, the one person in his life who prayed for him regularly and reminded him to pray. His regular visits to the "high church" chapel services at St. George's were tempered by Mrs. Everest's influence.

"Mrs. Everest was very much against the Pope," Churchill wrote. "She was herself Low Church, and her dislike of ornaments and ritual, and generally her extremely unfavourable opinion of the Supreme Pontiff, had prejudiced me strongly against that personage and all religious practices supposed to be associated with him. I therefore did not derive much comfort from the spiritual side of my education at this juncture. On the other hand, I experienced the fullest applications of the secular arm" by being beaten.

A younger student recorded that Winston was flogged at least once for stealing sugar from the pantry. Instead of being penitent after it was over, he kicked the headmaster's prized straw hat to pieces. After Winston left St. George's, boys heard that his "sojourn at the school had been one long feud with authority." Throughout his student years Winston would excel at subjects he liked and ignore those he didn't; no amount of punishment or other consequences could force him to concentrate on topics he found uninteresting or irrelevant.

After two years Jennie Jerome moved her son to another school, maybe in order to be near a good doctor. Winston was small for his age, tired easily, and could have had ear trouble that affected his balance. It's also possible that Mrs. Everest discovered lash marks where Winston had been flogged and told his mother about them. As an American, Jennie would have had little patience with the British tradition of such severe corporal punishment for young schoolboys.

From the pretentious world of St. George's, Winston moved at age nine to a school in Brighton run by two sisters, Kate and Charlotte Thomson. As a vacation resort on the southern coast of England, Brighton was famous for its healthful, bracing sea air. Winston thrived in the new surroundings, not only because of the weather but because instead of Latin and French he had more opportunity to study subjects that appealed to him. "I was allowed to learn things which interested me," he remembered, "French, History, lots of Poetry by heart, and above all Riding and Swimming. The impression of those years makes a pleasant picture in my mind, in strong contrast to my earlier schoolday memories."

Even before he left home for Ascot, Winston had developed the habit of writing faithfully to his mother and father from wherever he happened to be with Woomany. He continued this routine at St. George's and now at Brighton. Beginning with his first letter, written at age six, he said something almost every time about how much he missed his parents and wanted to see them. When were they coming? How long until the next vacation? Could they please send money or a basket of treats? He longed for their attention and affirmation. His mother visited seldom, his father almost never. Week after week it was Woom who traveled to the coast, took Winston on outings, and made sure he was well. In the meantime Lady Randolph busied herself with London society while Lord Randolph sailed to India on a junket intended to groom him for higher government office. They didn't concern themselves too much with the boys. That was the servant's job.

BRIGHTON AND HARROW

The new school in Brighton, so modest it didn't even have a name, gave nine-year-old Winston a fresh start. Every aspect of his life was different and better: more time spent outside, more subjects he enjoyed, an end to harsh corporal punishment. Ever-faithful Woom was still his only close adult contact and continued to shape his outlook on the world, especially on subjects important to her such as personal faith. She had made him precociously aware of religious symbolism and its power, which led to an early example of his independent thinking. Some would call it hardheadedness.

Students at the misses Thomsons' school went to church at the fashionable Chapel Royal in the middle of town. The pews there ran in sections parallel to the walls, all facing toward the center. On Winston's first visit, he and his classmates sat in pews facing west. When it came time to recite the Apostle's Creed, the whole congregation, regardless of where they sat, turned toward the east. Everyone, that is, except Winston. Convinced that Mrs. Everest would have considered the practice "Popish," he considered it his duty to stand fast, looking resolutely forward as everyone else in his section turned completely around to face the wall behind them.

"I was conscious of having created a 'sensation,'" he mused, and "prepared myself for martyrdom."[1] Such blatant behavior at St. George's would have earned him a brutal flogging. But when church was over and the students returned to school, no one said a word to Winston about what he'd done. He felt "almost disappointed" not to have suffered for his cause, and looked forward to the next Chapel Royal visit. But when that day came, the teachers seated their students in a different section of pews, facing east, so that when they recited the Creed, no one had to turn.

"I was puzzled to find my true course and duty," Churchill remembered. "It seemed excessive to turn away from the East. Indeed I could not feel that such a step would be justified. I therefore became willy-nilly a passive conformist. It was thoughtful and ingenious of these old ladies to have treated my scruples so tenderly. The results repaid their care. Never again have I caused or felt trouble on such a point. Not being resisted or ill-treated, I yielded myself complacently to a broad-minded tolerance and orthodoxy."[2]

It's hard to know how much of that sentiment he actually felt as a child and how much he added writing about the experience a generation later. But throughout his life Churchill remained a man of big ideas and broad strokes. He never fretted about the fine points of anything, including religious theology, practice, or belief. He developed into a panoramic thinker at every level, often unfamiliar with the details and always unconcerned with consistency, practicality, or implementation of the big idea whether it involved God, politics, war, or landscape architecture.

Winston did reasonably well at his studies in Brighton, placing in the top half of his class in every subject except mathematics. He acted in plays, continued with his riding and swimming, and wrote many, many letters to his parents and Woom. He nearly always begged them to come and see him, and frequently asked for money. There always seemed to be some reason for needing an extra shilling. He bought a stamp album and requested extra cash to offset this extravagance; he wanted a batch of school photos to trade with his friends. (Winston's picture shows a very young-looking boy in three-quarter left profile, dressed in an Eaton collar and derby hat.) Lord Randolph had built such a reputation as a speaker and parliamentary leader that Winston discovered there was a market for his autograph, and wrote his father, asking for copies of his signature to sell.

Winston sent out two types of letters: one was likely under a teacher's supervision and was in part a way to practice his handwriting; the other, far sloppier and more personal, were what he called "private letters" written on his own. Mrs. Everest came to visit in March 1886 and brought Winston's brother, Jack, along. Winston adored Jack even though it was clear to him that his younger brother was his mother's favorite because he was so easygoing and a diligent student; Winston, by comparison, was too independent minded and inattentive, too fond of attention. Woomy and the Churchill boys went to the beach and to restaurants, and had a wonderful time together. Winston wrote his mother, asking if they could stay a day or two longer. "It makes me feel so happy to think that my Oom and Jack are down here."

They did get to extend the visit, but soon after they left, Winston sent Mrs. Everest a heartfelt private letter, scarcely legible and covered with ink blots: "My dearest Oom, I recd. your letter. I am feeling very weak, I feel as if I could cry at every thing. I was all right after you left till just this evening. With love & kisses I remain yours affect. Winston."[3]

Soon after writing this undated note, Winston came down with pneumonia. For five days he lay near death, delirious, his temperature climbing above 104 degrees. Dr. Robson Roose attended him at his sickbed in Brighton and, in a sign of how dangerous the boy's condition was, Lord and Lady Randolph made the hour-and-twenty-minute rail journey from Victoria Station to be with him. Roose added a note of encouragement to the end of an early medical bulletin: "This report may appear grave yet it merely indicates the approach of the crisis which, please God, will result in an improved condition." Early the next morning he wrote an update: "At 2.15 a.m. the temp had fallen to 101, and now to 100, thank God. I shall give up my London work and stay by the boy today." A day later the doctor reported, "We have had a very anxious night but have managed to hold our own the temp is now 101 . . . your boy is making a wonderful fight and so I feel please God he will recover."

As Winston improved, the Churchills received sympathetic and encouraging notes from author Henry James, from the once and future prime minister Lord Salisbury on vacation in Monte Carlo, and from Lady Randolph's brother-in-law, Moreton Frewen, who sent greetings from the Prince of Wales at Buckingham Palace. Frewen also ventured a mild rebuke to Jennie for the way she had ignored her son in the past: "I hope

[Winston's illness] will leave no troublesome after effects, but even if it leaves him delicate for a long time to come you will make the more of him after being given back to you from the very threshold of the unknown."

Winston went home to London for a rest before returning to school and was recovered by summer vacation, though still frail and pale looking. Also that summer Lord Salisbury resumed the office of prime minister only six months after being voted out. (Under the British parliamentary system, the leader of a party becomes prime minister when that party is in power. Elections may be called anytime by the majority party, but no more than five years apart.) In August, Salisbury appointed Lord Randolph Chancellor of the Exchequer. The chancellorship was one of the most important and prestigious offices in the kingdom and marked Randolph, still only thirty-six, as a man destined for political greatness, almost certain to become prime minister within a few years. No one imagined at the time that this would be the high point of Randolph Churchill's parliamentary career.

Lord Randolph had already experienced periods of depression and exhaustion, behaving irrationally and showing flashes of anger that seemed to come out of nowhere. Victoria, who was queen when he was born and a personal friend of his parents, wrote in her diary that Randolph was "so mad and odd and also he has bad health." Churchill had scarcely settled into his cabinet post at the exchequer when he challenged the prime minister with a threat to resign in order to get his way on a relatively minor budget matter. Mindful of the need to keep the ruling party together, Lord Salisbury gave in. The same tactic worked again later;

Randolph seemed convinced that Salisbury would rather yield to him than take a chance on splitting the Conservative ranks.

Then, in December 1886, Randolph threatened to resign over a routine request for supplemental funding from the army. This time Salisbury resisted, and Randolph resigned just as he warned he would, confident that the prime minister wouldn't risk losing such a popular and successful parliamentarian as himself and would quickly change his mind. Randolph compounded the offense by neither getting the customary permission from the queen to resign nor consulting his wife, and by publishing his resignation letter in the *Times*. The queen declared, "The want of respect shown to me and to his colleagues have added to the bad effect which it produced." Jennie first learned of her husband's move in the newspaper. "He went into no explanation," she said of Lord Randolph the next morning at breakfast, "and I felt too utterly crushed and miserable to ask for any, or even to remonstrate." Though he sat in Parliament another eight years, he never held high office again. In forcing Salisbury's hand once too often, Randolph snuffed out his own future as a cabinet member after only five months.

For the time being, however, Lord and Lady Randolph continued with their social engagements and traveling as Winston prepared to leave Brighton for Harrow, an exclusive boys' boarding school in the countryside northwest of London. The Churchills traditionally attended Eaton, Harrow's archrival, but Winston went to Eaton because the higher terrain there supposedly produced a healthier climate. He was still small for his age, had little stamina, and had recurring trouble with his ears and eyes.

Winston's parents were on their way home from an excursion to Russia by way of Germany when he took the Harrow entrance exam. He and his Brighton teacher both decided he would have done better if he hadn't been so nervous. He passed, but only just "scraped through." Winston was sick after the tests were over, possibly out of a sense of relief that the deed was done, or because days later he came down with the mumps. Flat on his back once more, his biggest worry was missing Easter vacation at home. "I am so longing to see you my mummy," he wrote to Jennie. "My mumps are getting smaller every day. The very thought of going home is enough to draw them away."

Students from the Thomson sisters' school didn't usually go on to Harrow. The headmaster, the Reverend James Edward Cowell Welldon, may well have taken that (along with Lord Randolph's prominence) into consideration when accepting young Churchill for admission in April 1888 despite his borderline test scores. To help him make the transition from one school to another, Welldon assigned Winston to a small boarding house where he could get extra attention outside of class. And despite his low entrance marks, Winston did have the pleasure of reporting to his mother that his arithmetic grade was the highest of all the entrance papers.

Winston was slow to make friends. However, one memorable encounter that first year marked the beginning of a lifelong friendship. Harrow had a huge swimming pool, known as "the ducker," where the boys spent a lot of their spare time. "Naturally," Churchill admitted, "it was a good joke to come up behind some naked friend, or even enemy, and push him in. I made quite a habit of this with boys of my own size or less."

After only a month or so at Harrow, Winston spied a likely victim wrapped in a towel, sneaked up behind him, pulled off the towel, and shoved him in. To his horror, he quickly learned that the boy, Leo Amery, was three years older than he was, a gymnastics champion, and star of the soccer team. Churchill decided to make a preemptive move and ran to apologize, explaining he thought the boy was younger because he was so small. When Leo didn't consider that much of an excuse, Churchill "added in a most brilliant recovery, 'My father, who is a great man, is also small.'" Such quick thinking brought a laugh, Winston's apology was accepted, and the two became fast friends.

Amery played a role in Winston's "learning" his Latin translations. Churchill had always struggled with foreign languages while Leo, by contrast, could read Latin as well as English but had a hard time with English essays. Amery wrote Churchill's Latin translations and Churchill wrote Amery's essays. Amery went on to a career as a journalist, a member of Parliament, an industry executive, and more than fifty years after his surprise dunking, a member of Churchill's wartime cabinet.

His second year at Harrow, Winston moved to the headmaster's boarding house, larger and doubtless more prestigious. He had been anxious to make the move and finally asked his father to write the headmaster requesting it. Reverend Welldon answered Lord Randolph that "I should like to take him into my own House next term. He has some great gifts and is, I think, making progress in his work."[4]

This comment, even allowing for Victorian flattery toward a distinguished parent, reminds us that Churchill was not the academic dullard some historians have described. Churchill himself nurtured this impression later, pointing out that he was in the lowest section of the least accomplished students, "the third, or lowest division of the Fourth, or bottom, Form." He was no scholar at Harrow by any stretch, but he did well at anything that interested him, especially English and history.

Along with academic challenges there was the matter of his physical frailty and tendency to accidents. During his second year he was trying out a tricycle and, as he explained in a letter to his mother, "was used to a bicycle & turned too sharp," fell over, and had a concussion. Woom came to check on him every day as long as he was in bed. His mother visited Harrow only rarely, and it wasn't until the end of his second year that Lord Randolph found time to travel the ten miles from London to see his son at school.

For all his preoccupation with politics and society, Randolph stepped into Winston's life at crucial points. One of those times was when Winston was home for a visit, playing with his vast army of toy soldiers. His father asked him if he'd like to go into the army for real. When Winston said he would, Lord Randolph wrote Reverend Welldon that he should put Winston in the army class, which was for boys interested in preparing for military training. Churchill remarked that "the toy soldiers turned the current of my life. Henceforth all my education was directed to passing into Sandhurst [the military academy], and afterwards to the technical details of the profession of arms. Anything else I had to pick up myself."

Upper-crust British society considered only a few occupations as socially acceptable. Lord Randolph drew no salary as a politician but lived off his marriage settlement. His father, and later his older brother, depended on income from the ducal estate. The military, the church, and the law were the only wage-earning positions deemed proper for the grandson of a duke. Evidently Lord Randolph believed Winston was not smart enough to be a lawyer, and would likely never have even considered the church. That left the military, and since the boy seemed interested in soldiers and battle tactics, the matter was settled as far as Randolph was concerned.

Winston displayed his early enthusiasm for the idea in an essay he wrote at age fourteen, the same year he joined the army class. Eighteen hundred words long, it was a first-person account of an imaginary battle between British and Russian troops written in grand classical style, filled with history and heroics, and illustrated with large maps. His teacher saved it because it was so remarkable, further proof that when the topic interested him, Winston excelled in his performance. Comments on his report card that year support this conclusion. He was "fair" in French and "rather slow" in chemistry, "not brilliant but works well" in math. In history he wrote "very intelligently," and overall, his tutor reported, "has considerable power of application and is very intelligent. He is getting on nicely."

He may have been small and delicate, but Winston had plenty of grit and physical determination. His medical troubles continued—he saw doctors about difficulties with his teeth and eyes, leg pains, and what was evidently a hernia—yet he was a member of Harrow's victorious swim team and also won shooting and fencing competitions. He would go on to become private school fencing champion in 1892. That year he wrote home excitedly, "I have won the fencing. A very fine cup. I was far and away first. Absolutely untouched in the finals."[5] The school paper, the *Harrovian*, reported that his success "was chiefly due to his quick and dashing attack which quite took his opponents by surprise. . . . Churchill must be congratulated on his success over all his opponents in the fencing line, many of whom must have been much taller and more formidable than himself."[6]

Despite his upbeat report card, there were periods when his work was so unsatisfactory he had to turn it in to his tutor or the headmaster every week along with the instructor's comments. When he was having a hard time, Woomey was his great confidante and consolation. By contrast he got little encouragement from his parents. In a letter from 1890, Jennie scolded, "Dearest Winston you make me very unhappy—I had built up such hopes about you—& now all is gone. My only consolation is that your conduct is good, & that you are an affectionate son—but your work is an insult to your intelligence."[7]

There are many historical accounts of Winston's passing interest in a career in the church. One of the few solid clues about his feeling and motivation comes from a widely quoted postscript in a letter written to his mother from school on July 13, 1891: "Really I feel less keen about the Army every day. I think the church would suit me better."[8] But the motive here was probably more about escaping a summer of foreign language study than about being called into the ministry. Reverend Welldon had suggested to Lady Randolph that Winston spend the upcoming summer vacationing in France with a French family to improve his language skills. Winston was horrified at the idea, which meant he couldn't spend the time with his brother, his mother, and Woom (his father was in South Africa). This postscript was in Winston's letter back to his mother, begging her not to make him go, but to hire a French servant for the summer instead. "A governess would I am sure answer all the immediate colloquial requirements," he argued, and "I beg you to let me have a bit of fun."

Though Winston did in fact talk over the prospect of studying for the clergy on other occasions, it seems unlikely that he had any real interest or inclination in that direction. His was more the typical musing and thinking out loud any boy in his midteens might go through when wondering about his future. His P.S. to his mother was more likely a ploy to avoid a summer in France than any deeply felt commitment to holy orders. Within days he would forget about it completely.

Beyond his christening, his parents gave no thought to his religious development either. When Lady Randolph told her husband that Winston was going in for his confirmation that fall, she, too, suspected his motives. "Perhaps it will steady him," she wrote. "Welldon wrote that Winston wished to become a candidate [for the ministry]—I'm afraid only because it will get him off other work!" That summer at home Winston had been a handful for her: "On the whole he has been a very good boy—but honestly he is getting a bit too old for a woman to manage. After all he will be 17 in 2 months and he really requires to be with a man."

In typical fashion Mrs. Everest was delighted at Winston's confirmation and kept up her interest in his spiritual development. "I am so glad to hear you are going to be confirmed," she wrote, making immediate plans to attend. "When is it to be my Angel?" The ceremony was held in the chapel at Harrow, suitably Gothic with a high-beamed ceiling and rich stained-glass windows. Winston took communion that day for the only time in his life.

Woom encouraged Winston to make a good impression on his parents, work hard, and reach out to God. "I hope you will try & work well dearest this term to please His Lordship on his return & your Mamma has given you every pleasure and indulgence she could these holidays so I am sure you will try & do your best to please them & disappoint some of your relations who prophesy a future of profligacy for you. I trust you will be kept from all evil and temptation. I will pray for you & don't forget to pray hourly to be kept my sweet precious dear Boy."

Winston had taken the preliminary entrance exam for Sandhurst, one of the two British military academies, in November 1890, after Reverend Welldon advised him to postpone it from the summer to give him more time to get ready. When the results were announced, Winston was one of only twelve of the twenty-nine Harrovians taking the test who passed every subject. He was beside himself with delight. But two years later, working on the civil service examination for actual admission to the academy, the outcome was disappointing: Winston had failed. This was not unusual, as many applicants took the exam more than once. That meant that, although he should have graduated at the end of the term, Winston came back to Harrow in the fall to retake the test.

Results of the second exam would not be announced until January. Winston went home to London to await the news, nervous but hopeful. The turn of the new year, 1893, marked the beginning of one of the most important and tumultuous seasons in Winston Churchill's life.

SANDHURST

Winston spent Christmas at his aunt Lady Wimbourne's estate on the coast at Bournemouth because there wasn't really anyplace else to go. He'd missed visiting his beloved Blenheim since his grandfather died and his ill-tempered uncle became the eighth duke of Marlborough. He couldn't go home to his parents' house in London because they had moved in with his grandmother to save money. Lord Randolph was a serious gambler at Monte Carlo and the racetrack and had lost heavily, contributing to his chronic habit of overspending to maintain a lifestyle appropriate to his social and political status.

On January 10, 1893, Winston was playing chase with Jack and their cousin. He ran onto a footbridge across a deep ravine and got trapped between pursuers at each end. Looking down, he saw the tops of trees growing up from the bottom of the ravine and calculated he could jump onto one of them safely, avoiding the indignity of being captured by the younger boys. Winston went over the side—and fell twenty-nine feet to the ground.

He lay unconscious for three days with a concussion (his third, after the donkey in Dublin and the tricycle at Harrow), back injuries, and a ruptured kidney. His father hurried to Bournemouth and brought the best London doctors with him. Winston spent weeks in bed, which was also when he learned he'd failed his second admission exam to the military academy.

This time Reverend Welldon recommended Winston go to a "crammer," a teacher who specialized in cram courses for boys trying get into Sandhurst or Woolwich, the two royal military academies. It was not rare for a student to need such a level of help, and this particular crammer, Captain Walter H. James, was famous for being able to get even the toughest cases successfully passed into the academies. Six weeks after his accident, Winston started in with Captain James, who immediately recognized his intelligence but felt he wasn't trying very hard. "I had to speak to him the other day about his casual manner," he reported to Lord Randolph. Winston, the captain observed, "means well but he is distinctly inclined to be inattentive and to think too much of his abilities."[1] For example, Winston told the captain he knew quite enough history and didn't need to learn any more. He took the entrance exam for the third time in June, then, while waiting for the results, went on a walking tour of Switzerland with Jack and their tutor.

The travelers were on their way to Lucerne when Winston got word he had passed. His entrance score wasn't high enough to get into the infantry, which is where his father wanted him and where he'd already used his influence to get his son a position, but Winston preferred the cavalry anyway. "I was delighted at having passed the examination," he said, "and even more at the prospect of soldiering on horseback. I had already formed a definite opinion upon the relative advantages of riding and walking. What fun it would be having a horse! Also the uniforms of the cavalry were far more magnificent then those of the Foot." Winston still loved riding and continued to excel at it. This coupled with his delicate health made the cavalry a clear favorite.

Churchill failed to get into the infantry not because their standards were higher, but because more applicants wanted to join the infantry than the cavalry. Cadets generally tended to shy away from the cavalry for the very reason Randolph didn't want Winston there: it was expensive. Cavalry officers didn't earn nearly enough to afford the regal uniforms, equipment, and other trappings they were expected to maintain, and so had to buy them with their own money. The financial burden on infantry officers was far less.

Winston proudly wrote to his father, who was taking the waters at the world-renowned Bavarian health resort of Bad Kissingen, a favorite of Imperial Chancellor Bismark, Czar Alexander of Russia, and other European nobles. To his shock and disappointment, he received a scathing answer in return. Though they were never close, Winston had always idolized his father from afar, admiring him for his popularity and deeply proud of his political successes. Randolph's letter must have broken his heart:

> The first extremely discreditable feature of your performance
> was missing the infantry, for in that failure is demonstrated
> beyond refutation your slovenly happy-go-lucky harum scarum
> style of work for which you have always been distinguished. . . .

The second discreditable fact in the result of your examination is that you have not perceptively increased as far as my memory serves the marks you made in the examination. . . . You may find some consolation that you have failed to get into the "60th Rifles," one of the finest regiments in the army. There is another satisfaction for you in that by accomplishing the prodigious effort of getting into the Cavalry, you imposed on me an extra charge of some £200 a year. Not that I shall allow you to remain in the Cavalry. As soon as possible I shall arrange your exchange into an infantry regiment of the line . . . you need not trouble to write any answer to this part of my letter, because I no longer attach the slightest weight to anything you may say about your own acquirements & exploits . . . if your conduct and action at Sandhurst is similar to what it has been in the other establishments . . . then my responsibility for you is over. . . . You will become a mere social wastrel, one of the hundreds of the public school failures, and you will degenerate into a shabby unhappy & futile existence.[2]

The perspective of history clarifies a reason for Lord Randolph's seemingly inexcusable criticism: he was going insane. In less than a year and a half he would be dead at age forty-five. Only a year earlier Winston had a treasured private conversation with his father, who had reprimanded him then for shooting off a loud gun outside his window, then softened when he saw how hard his rebuke had stung. Churchill recalled:

He explained how old people were not always very considerate towards young people that they were absorbed in their

own affairs and might well speak roughly in sudden annoy-
ance. . . . He proceeded to talk to me in the most wonderful
and captivating manner about school and going into the Army
and the grown-up life which lay beyond. I listened spellbound
to this sudden complete departure from his usual reserve,
amazed at his intimate comprehension of all my affairs. Then
at the end he said, "Do remember things do not always go
right with me. My every action is misjudged and every word
distorted. . . . So make some allowances."

By the time he entered Sandhurst in the fall of 1893, Winston
had seen enough erratic and unusual behavior in his father to
know something wasn't right. Lord Randolph's temper was
mercurial and unpredictable. Still a member of Parliament even
though he had no cabinet office, he gave speeches that now had
none of his old fire and popular appeal. Whether in the House
of Commons or in public, his listeners had stopped paying attention and stopped caring.

It was a hard season for Winston as his father struggled.
Lord Randolph's debts continued to mount, his political influence to wane, and his health to decline. The family financial
straits even prompted the Churchills in essence to dismiss Mrs.
Everest, telling her there wasn't room for her when they moved
in with the duchess at her London home. Winston did finally
convince his parents to at least send Woomy some money for
living expenses.

As it turned out, Winston could join the infantry after all
because several candidates who won places had decided to not
take them. He still preferred the cavalry and managed to hang

on to his preference in spite of his father's earlier objection. He even secured an allowance of £10 a month from Lord Randolph (worth around $1,200 today), plus his tailor and haberdasher bills on top of that. Despite this seeming generosity, Winston was constantly short of cash and ended up taking six years to pay for his uniforms, which were quite elaborate and impressive, immaculately fitted, covered with gold braid, and accented with high boots and a sealskin busby smaller than but similar to the famous bearskin hats of the Coldstream Guards.

Consistent with his past academic career, he shined brightly when he felt the topic was interesting or useful, and fell to the bottom when he didn't. In 1894 he finished second in his class of 127 in the riding exam. That year he also saw a famous throat specialist, Sir Felix Semon, asking him to "cure the impediment in my speech, please."[3] All his life he had had trouble saying the letter *s*, producing a sort of hissing lisp. His interest in correcting it is evidence that even at this early date he was thinking of following his father into politics and setting his sights high. "I'm going into the army first," he informed Sir Felix. "But as a [cabinet] minister later, I can't be haunted by the idea that I must avoid every word beginning with an s."[4]

The doctor gave Winston exercises to soften his impediment such as, "The Spanish ships I cannot see for they are not in sight." Though scarcely out of his teens, Churchill cut an impressive figure even with so distinguished a man as Sir Felix. Commenting on the young cadet he wrote, "I have just seen the most extraordinary young man I have ever met."[5]

The adventure of Prudes on the Prowl that summer demonstrates how Churchill was also already making a name for himself as a man of action with a knack for inspiring a crowd and commanding the headlines. Sandhurst cadets' weekly leave ran from noon Saturday to midnight Sunday. Many men spent the weekend in London at the theaters and music halls, partying late into the night to squeeze every drop of enjoyment out of their time. Mrs. Ormiston Chant, of the London city council, decided Saturday nights were getting out of hand, particularly at the popular Empire Theater where young people congregated for drinks and conversation.

Mrs. Chant started a campaign to close the Empire bars. The London *Daily Telegraph* made fun of the idea in a series of articles titled "Prudes on the Prowl," while the cadets and other young adults vigorously protested this attempt to shut down one of their favorite gathering places. Churchill considered the move "entirely uncalled-for and contrary to the best traditions of British freedom."[6]

Winston wrote a letter to the *Westminster Gazette* that was published, making it his first work to ever appear in print, declaring that "improvement in the standard of public decency is due rather to improved social conditions and to the spread of education than to the prowling of the prudes. . . . The only method of reforming human nature and of obtaining a higher standard of morality is by educating the mind of the individual and improving the social conditions under which he lives." The letter received widespread attention.

In what Winston hailed as a "characteristically British compromise," Mrs. Chant and her backers agreed to leave the bars open, separating them from the theater lobby with a light canvas screen, dividing them completely except at openings left as doorways and for ventilation. "Thus," Churchill observed, "the temples of Venus and Bacchus, though adjacent, would be separated, and their attack upon human frailties could only be delivered in a successive or alternating and not in concentrated form."

The next Saturday night as the lobby filled with young men and women, someone gave a section of the canvas a defiant yank. In minutes the theater was a shambles as the whole screen around the lobby perimeter came crashing down. Energized and inspired by this bold and spontaneous strike in the name of freedom, Winston Churchill made his first public speech. As he recounted the moment, "Mounting on the debris and indeed partially emerging from it, I addressed the tumultuous crowd. . . . I discarded the constitutional argument entirely and appealed directly to sentiment and even to passion, finishing up by saying, 'You have seen us tear down these barricades to-night; see that you pull down those who are responsible for them at the coming election.' These words were received with rapturous applause, and we all sallied out into the Square brandishing fragments of wood and canvas as trophies or symbols." Churchill and the other cadets then led a triumphant public protest but a short-lived one: they had to catch the last train back to Sandhurst.

Winston's military training continued as his parents lived more and more separate lives. Increasingly unstable Lord Randolph took long vacations with male friends, which raised eyebrows in polite society. Meanwhile Jennie's many love affairs had become an open secret. She was beautiful, outgoing, and self-confident in a way British women seldom were, and enjoyed the attentions of men. Her husband was often away, and when he was home he behaved so unpredictably she never knew what to expect. His political career was in decline, he had lost a fortune gambling, and most of their income was from her side of the family anyway. Jennie wanted more out of life and wasn't shy about reaching for it.

One member of her social circle ventured a guess that she entertained two hundred different lovers in her lifetime, beginning with officers and noblemen on her father-in-law's staff when he was viceroy of Ireland. Her favorite was Count Charles Rudolph Kinsky, an Austrian diplomat in London and a friend of Lord Randolph's. Society took her liaisons in stride, as apparently did Winston, who even stumbled upon his mother and the count having breakfast in a hotel. Kinsky and Winston had something of an uncle/nephew relationship. The count took Winston on outings, sent him stamps for his collection, and otherwise went out of his way to reach out to him, which Winston appreciated.

Lord Randolph's irrational temper flared when Winston damaged a valuable pocket watch his father had given him. Randolph happened to see it in for repair at the watchmaker's and wrote to his son that the watchmaker told him Winston had dropped it in the water. "I would not believe you could be such a young stupid. It is clear you are not to be trusted with a valuable watch. . . . Jack has the watch I gave him longer than you have had yours . . . in all qualities of steadiness taking care of his things & never doing stupid things Jack is vastly your superior."

Contrary to his father's belief, Winston had taken extraordinary measures on account of the watch. It had slipped out of his breast pocket when he leaned over a stream running through the academy. He dived in after it but couldn't find it. The next day he had the stream dredged without success, so he and nearly two dozen other cadets rerouted the stream and pumped the original bed dry with a fire engine—all of which Winston paid for—to retrieve the watch.

Lord Randolph's doctor insisted he take a complete rest. When he refused, the doctor proposed he take a trip around the world instead. In June 1894 Lord and Lady Randolph sailed for America, traveling with the son of one of the family doctors. Winston, Jack, and their tutor spent another summer in Europe.

In San Francisco the Churchills had their photographs taken. Jennie is dressed in a crisp pleated blouse with a fashionable coat or cape over her shoulders, a bit of a curl in her hair and the hint of a smile on her lips. Lord Randolph looks off with a vacant stare, his eyes half-open, his mouth emotionless beneath his waxed moustache. Jennie's letters to her sister Leonie reveal her worry over her husband's condition. "I dread the chance of even seeing people for his sake." "He is quite unfit for society . . . it was dreadful being with strangers." "You cannot imagine anything more distracting & desperate than to watch him & see him as he is & to think of him as he was."[7] On top of the stress of dealing with Randolph, she received a telegram saying her beloved Count Kinsky, tired of waiting for her, had become engaged. "I HATE IT," she wrote her sister. "I shall return without a friend in the world & too old to make any more now."[8]

The Churchills came home to London on Christmas Eve. Lord Randolph died early in the morning of January 24, 1895, with Winston and the rest of the family around him. "His end was quite painless," Winston said.[9] Days later he was buried at Bladon churchyard near Blenheim.

The cause of Lord Randolph's death still sparks arguments

among historians. Many insist there is virtually no doubt he died of syphilis, while some are equally convinced that he had a brain tumor. Based on the symptoms reported, multiple sclerosis is another possibility. The fact is, during a time when medical science was relatively primitive, it's impossible to say without reservation how someone met his end. At the time, his doctors and family were convinced it was syphilis. Only more recently has a group of historians, some with blood ties to Lord Randolph, theorized that the syphilis story was fabricated later to embarrass Winston politically and that "based on a reassessment of all the available facts" death was by "a deep-seated tumor of the brain."[10]

Randolph's doctors included a specialist in venereal disease, and the facts surrounding his case were couched in terms of Victorian propriety. When his friend the Prince of Wales asked his own physician what was wrong with Lord Randolph, the doctor reported he told what he thought could be "communicated *without indiscretion.*" Winston convinced his own doctor to tell him what was going on, and promised his mother "I shall never tell anyone." Jennie poured out her heart in a letter to her sister. "Up to now the General Public and even Society does not know the real truth, and after *all* my sacrifices and the misery of these six months it would be hard if it got out. It would do incalculable harm to his political reputation and memory and is a dreadful thing for all of us."

What is certain is that Lord Randolph's symptoms were in every way consistent with syphilis: periods of incoherence, violent outbursts (in Yokohama he tried to kill his valet), delusion, apathy. Once contracted, the disease can lie dormant for years, then goes to work destroying the central nervous system.

Various stories from relatives and others who knew him well suggest he caught the disease from either a prostitute during college, a mistress in Paris, or a chambermaid at Blenheim. His doctor listed the cause of death as "general paralysis of the insane," the euphemism of the time for syphilis.

Winston scarcely had time to absorb the shock of these events when in July dear old Woomy passed away. She had spent her last two years living with the family who had employed her before the Churchills had, an archbishop and his wife. Winston was beside her when she died. He had lost, he said, "my dearest and most intimate friend during the whole of the twenty years I had lived."[11]

We know little about Elizabeth Ann Everest, not even her date of birth. Yet what a mark she made on the world! Her boy Winston would grow up to become one of the great heroes of the twentieth century, with a sense of responsibility, honor, and moral courage that inspired millions. He could scarcely have acquired those characteristics from his parents, though his mother did become much more a part of his life after Lord Randolph died and Winston finished his schooling. He didn't get them in any quantity from teachers or friends. Rather it was Mrs. Everest, dear old Oom, who shaped his moral character more than anybody. She was the one who prayed for him often and encouraged him to pray. She came to his confirmation, attended his plays and concerts, and connected with him on an emotional and spiritual level no other person even came close to as long as she was alive.

"Death came very easy to her," Winston wrote of her last hours. "She had lived such an innocent and loving life of service to others and held such a simple faith, that she had no fears at all, and did not seem to mind very much."[12] Whatever seeds of moral guidance, interest in spiritual matters, or reflections on Christianity had been planted in Winston Churchill by the day he graduated twentieth out of 130 from Sandhurst, a poor old maid nanny had put them there.

Eager for action, Winston joined his cavalry regiment, the 4th Hussars, stationed at a large military installation in Aldershot, south of London. The unit was preparing for a six-year rotation in Bangalore, India, by tradition taking its turn keeping the peace in the far reaches of the British Empire. This was not an auspicious time for young officers itching for battle. Britain hadn't been involved in a war of any consequence with a foreign power since the Crimean War against Russia forty years before. Heading into the twentieth century, some military experts thought warfare had become obsolete and that modern nations would never engage in full-scale conflict.

Churchill soon made his own adventure, to the envy of his friends.

ANGLING FOR
ADVENTURE

arracks life with the 4th Hussars at Aldershot was boring, ill suited for a young man bent on military action. Churchill soon started angling for adventure and in the process established a pattern of behavior that served him well for years to come. There was armed conflict under way in Cuba, where the native population was rising up against their imperial Spanish overseers. Eager to get in on the action somehow even though the English were not officially involved, Winston wrote to his mother, asking her to use her influence to get him permission to go to Cuba while his unit was waiting to be deployed to India. "This is a pushing age," he told her, "and we must shove with the best."[1] His perspective was the perfect complement to his mother's view, which was, "Do business, darling, only at the top."

Still a beauty in her early forties, Jennie Churchill had a host of connections, political acquaintances, and lovers to call on for favors on behalf of her older son. She got Winston permission to leave the cavalry temporarily and to attach himself as a non-combatant to the Spanish army in Cuba, landing him an assignment writing articles about the war for the London *Daily Graphic*. Extraordinary leeway and privileged access on account of his mother's connections, plus an income from writing to help pay for it all—these were the ingredients Churchill used time and again to get to the center of the action.

Churchill and a fellow officer sailed to New York, where one of his mother's lovers, a politician and society figure named Bourke Cockrane, arranged for a private railroad car to take them to Florida; there they caught a boat for the short voyage to Havana. Cockrane and Winston got along well; in fact Churchill said years later that he copied his famous speaking style from the florid and expansive New Yorker.

In spite of the tropical heat, insects, and long days in the saddle, Churchill was elated to be riding with the Spanish army on patrol for Cuban rebels. The discomfort was worth it, he thought, because a soldier who had been under fire "had an aura about him to which the Generals he served under, the troopers he led, and the girls he courted, accorded a unanimous, sincere, and spontaneous recognition." He marked his twenty-first birthday by being shot at for the first time. It was the high adventure he had longed for. As he saw it, "To travel thousands of miles with money one could ill afford, and get up at four o'clock in the morning in the hope of getting into a scrape in the company of perfect strangers, is certainly hardly a rational proceeding. Yet we knew there were very few subalterns in the British Army who would not have given a month's pay to sit in out saddles." Despite his official status as an observer and reporter, the Spanish

awarded him a Cuban campaign medal, though as a British officer he wasn't allowed to wear it. He could only hope there would
be more excitement ahead with his regiment.

Over the next three years Churchill found plenty of excitement, but not around the colonial garrison in Bangalore, a large,
hot, inland city in southwestern India. He went out of his way
to go where the fighting was, sometimes raising the hackles of
his superiors because of the favors his mother, or respect for his
father's memory, gained him in high places. During the year or
so of that time he was actually in Bangalore, he used the long
afternoon siestas, when all work and training stopped because
of the blistering heat, to tackle an ambitious reading program
that would make up for his lack of a university education. He
also reflected on his experiences in the cavalry as they unfolded
and sometimes thought about them in uncharacteristically deep
and spiritual ways. Being a soldier in combat, coming face-
to-face with death, knowing any day might be his last—these
realities led him consciously to consider matters of faith with
new seriousness.

One early example of this experience-then-reflection came
the very day Winston arrived in India, landing at the huge,
bustling port of Calcutta. Eager to get ashore, he and a few
other officers hired a small boat to take them from their ship
to the dock ahead of the others. As he climbed out of the boat,
Winston grabbed a large iron ring in the side of the quay. Just as
he took hold, the boat dropped suddenly, pulling his right shoulder out of its socket. Painful and crippling as it was, he didn't get
immediate attention because there was too much in this exotic
place to see and do to waste time on a doctor. He eventually had

his shoulder treated, but it bothered him the rest of his life. He strapped the arm to his side when he played polo, and even many years later had to be careful when gesturing as he spoke so as to not dislocate the shoulder again.

His philosophizing about the injury yields a peek at the wider worldview he was forming: "This accident was a serious piece of bad luck. However, you never can tell whether bad luck may not after all turn out to be good luck. . . . One must never forget when misfortunes come that it is quite possible they are saving one from something much worse; or that when you make some great mistake, it may very easily serve you better than the best-advised decision. Life is a whole, and luck is a whole, and no part of them can be separated from the rest."[2]

At age twenty-one, Churchill was pondering the question of what it is that rules men's lives. Is it luck? Fortune? The power of individual decisions? His intellect and experience guided him toward acknowledging some kind of life-directing force. He didn't see it as Christianity or any religion at all; that wasn't a frame of reference he was familiar with. But he sensed something was there.

Over the next several months, the wheels kept turning. Winston recalled a friend telling him before he left England that the gospel of Christ was "the last word in Ethics." The gospel and ethics all sounded good, but he didn't actually know what ethics were. He'd learned nothing of them at Harrow or Sandhurst. "Judging from the context," he guessed, "I thought they must mean 'the public school spirit,' 'playing the game,' 'esprit de corps,' 'honourable behaviour,' 'patriotism,' and the like." Someone explained to him that ethics consisted not only of what a person ought to do but why he or she should do it, "and that there were whole books written on the subject."[3]

He said he would gladly have paid for a scholarly lecture on ethics but in Bangalore there was no one to give it. "Of tactics I had a grip: on politics I had a view: but a concise compendious outline of Ethics was a novelty not to be locally obtained."

If an ethics expert wasn't available, there were plenty of other topics to consider during week after week of long, hot tropical afternoons. Winston read history first of all, particularly weighty standards including all eight volumes of *The Decline and Fall of the Roman Empire* by Edward Gibbon, and the twelve-volume *History of England* by Thomas Macaulay. He also studied, among many other authors, Plato and Aristotle; Blaise Pascal, whose religious philosophy that man in nature was "a nothing in relation to infinity" laid the groundwork for existentialism; and Charles Darwin, whose evolutionary theory pointed toward random selection rather than a divine creator.

Reading and analyzing the works of these great minds prompted Churchill to ask himself probing questions about religion. Until then he, by his own admission, had never thought much about the matter but rather "dutifully accepted everything I had been told."[4] As a student he was marched into chapel regularly, and at home on holidays had typically gone to church once a week, especially if Mrs. Everest had anything to say about it.

The army encouraged church attendance, and sometimes as a subaltern—a junior officer roughly equivalent to a lieutenant—Churchill marched soldiers to church, both Roman Catholic and Protestant. There was far more religious diversity in the British army than in British society. To Churchill, religious tolerance in the military was so broad it "had spread till it overlapped the regions of indifference." Soldiers were free to worship as they wished, and everyone was furnished with facilities for their religious practices, whether Western or Eastern.

Native Indian religions prompted lively discussions among the British troops. Churchill noted:

> In the regiment we sometimes used to argue questions like "Whether we should live again in another world after this was over?" "Whether we have ever lived before?" "Whether we remember and meet each other after Death or merely start again like the Buddhists?" "Whether some high intelligence is looking after the world or whether things are just drifting on anyhow?" There was general agreement that if you tried your best to live an honourable life and did your duty and were faithful to friends and not unkind to the weak and poor, it did not matter much what you believed or disbelieved. All would come out all right.

Churchill concluded, "This is what would nowadays I suppose be called 'The Religion of Healthy-Mindedness.'"

Churchill was a man of action, who seldom stopped for introspection or careful analysis, even about deep subjects. He believed "a man's Life must be nailed to a cross either of Thought or Action" and came down unequivocally on the side of action. Only during this relatively inactive time in his life, when he was reading and thinking so diligently, did he delve more fully into matters of destiny, spirituality, and religious practice.

Senior officers in his regiment said Christianity had its

strong points for certain segments of the population and certain circumstances. Christianity was good for women, the officers thought, because it "helps to keep them straight." It was also good for the poor and marginalized of society, what Churchill called "the lower orders," because faith made their hard life more bearable by promising a better time in the hereafter, making them less demanding, more docile, and therefore easier to manage in the present.

Christianity, Churchill said, "had also a disciplinary value, especially when presented through the Church of England. It made people want to be respectable, to keep up appearances, and so saved lots of scandals." This raises a question Churchill and his fellow officers evidently never considered. According to them, if you lived an honorable life and did your duty, everything would be fine. But honorable according to what standard? Dutiful by what gauge? What identifies a woman's behavior as straight? Respectable by whose reckoning? These men and their culture had a shared moral compass so deeply embedded they didn't even recognize it, one set according to centuries of Christian belief and practice.

Yet to Subaltern Winston Churchill the traditions of the church, which he'd observed week after week, year after year as a student, were pointless "ceremonies and ritual. They were merely the same idea translated into different languages to suit different races and temperaments." Too much religion "of any kind" was a bad thing, Churchill decided, particularly the violent Islamic element. "Among natives especially, fanaticism was highly dangerous and roused them to murder, mutiny or rebellion."

In this climate of religious thinking and inquiry, Churchill started reading books that he realized "challenged the whole religious education I had received at Harrow." The first of them was *The Martyrdom of Man* by Winwood Reade, a war correspondent for the London *Times* in Africa, self-proclaimed disciple of Charles Darwin, variously described as agnostic, anti-Catholic, and atheist, who asserted there was no afterlife. Reade believed that man was not on earth to prepare for a better life in heaven but to subdue the earth for his own use "that he might exalt his intellectual and moral powers until he had gained perfection." Man, not God, was the source of man's goodness.

To Winston it was "a concise and well-written universal history of mankind, dealing in harsh terms with the mysteries of all religions and leading to the depressing conclusion that we simply go out like candles. I was much startled and indeed offended by what I read." Reflecting further, however, Churchill found reinforcement for Reade's views in Gibbon and also in William Lecky's *Rise and Influence of Rationalism* and *History of European Morals*, both of which he said "established in my mind a predominately secular view." Lecky warned against taking any pastor's or congregation's word for anything unless the hearer believed it in his own mind.

His intellectual curiosity piqued, Winston wished he had a broader survey of the study of religion available in Bangalore. "For a time I was indignant at having been told so many untruths, as I then regarded them, by the schoolmasters and clergy who had guided my youth. Of course if I had been at a University my difficulties might have been resolved by the eminent professors and divines who are gathered there. At any rate, they would have shown me equally convincing books putting the opposite point of view."

Thinkers and writers of every stripe have made endless effort over the years to line up religious points of view with religious experience: If you say you believe this, then you should do that. If this is your faith, then that is the conclusion you must draw from events as they unfold. If you hold this view intellectually, then you of course hold that view spiritually. With refreshing honesty, Churchill decided he didn't really care about tying the head to the heart in matters of religion and that it didn't really matter.

Churchill considered his army experience, and these months in Bangalore in particular, a crucial time in establishing his personal view of religion. "I passed through a violent and aggressive anti-religious phase which, had it lasted, might easily have made me a nuisance," he wrote in *My Early Life*.

> My poise was restored during the next few years by frequent contact with danger. I found that whatever I might think and argue, I did not hesitate to ask for special protection when about to come under the fire of the enemy: nor to feel sincerely grateful when I got home safe to tea. I even asked for lesser things than not to be killed too soon, and nearly always in these years, and indeed throughout my life, I got what I wanted. This practice seemed perfectly natural, and just as strong and real as the reasoning process which contradicted it so sharply. Moreover the practice was comforting and the reasoning led nowhere. I therefore acted in accordance with my feelings without troubling to square such conduct with the conclusions of thought.

This pegs Churchill as something of a foxhole convert, but he would see nothing wrong with that. Though he readily admitted his heart appealed to God in moments of danger on the battlefield, he didn't feel intellectually obliged to accept the whole Christianity package. Intellectual skepticism shouldn't keep someone from feeling free to reach out to God for protection, and conversely, making that emotional appeal shouldn't obligate a person to accept a belief he considers irrational. There was no reason why the heart and the head had to act in tandem.

Churchill came across a quotation by Blaise Paschal that perfectly expressed his viewpoint: "*Le Coeur a ses raisons, que la raison ne connait pas.*" ("The heart has its reasons that reason knows nothing of." The passage continues: "We feel it in a thousand things. It is the heart which experiences God, and not the reason. This, then, is faith: God felt by the heart, not by the reason.")

Churchill remarked:

> It seemed to me that it would be very foolish to discard the reasons of the heart for those of the head. Indeed I could not see why I should not enjoy them both. I did not worry about the inconsistency of thinking one way and believing the other. It seemed good to let the mind explore so far as it could the paths of thought and logic, and also good to pray for help and succour, and be thankful when they came. I could not feel that the Supreme Creator who gave us minds as well as our souls would be offended if they did not always run smoothly together in double harness. After all He must have foreseen this from the beginning and of course He would understand it all.

To Churchill the essential aspect of faith was its effect, not its source, form, or origins. Arguments about the latter were a waste of time.

> Accordingly I have always been surprised to see some of our Bishops and clergy making such heavy weather about reconciling the Bible story with modern scientific and historical knowledge. Why do they want to reconcile them? If you are the recipient of a message which cheers your heart and fortifies your soul, which promises you reunion with those you have loved in a world of larger opportunity and wider sympathies, why should you worry about the shape or colour of the travel-stained envelope; whether it is duly stamped, whether the date on the postmark is right or wrong? These matters may be puzzling, but they are certainly not important. What is important is the message and the benefits to you of receiving it.

Did Christ actually walk on water and turn water into wine? To Winston the answer was irrelevant, and requiring every affirmation of faith to pass a test of reason or intellect was itself unreasonable even in the modern age.

> Close reasoning can conduct one to the precise conclusion that miracles are impossible: that "it is much more likely that human testimony should err, than that the laws of nature should be violated;" and at the same time one may rejoice to read how Christ turned the water into wine in Cana of Galilee or walked of the lake or rose from the dead. The human brain cannot comprehend infinity, but the discovery of mathematics

enables it to be handled quite easily. The idea that nothing is true except that we comprehend is silly, and that ideas which our minds cannot reconcile are mutually destructive, sillier still. Certainly nothing could be more repulsive both to our minds and feelings than the spectacle of thousands of millions of universes—for that is what they say it comes to now—all knocking about together for ever without any rational or good purpose behind them. I therefore adopted quite early in life a system of believing whatever I wanted to believe, while at the same time leaving reason to pursue unfettered whatever paths she was capable of treading.

This attitude seemingly gave Winston Churchill all the benefits of Christianity with none of the liabilities. He could call on God for help when he was in trouble, but otherwise believe whatever he wanted to believe and live as he wanted to live. And what he came to believe in more than anything, at least in his public persona, was himself. Author Gretchen Ruben concluded that this heroic self-assurance made Churchill's history-making accomplishments possible. In *Forty Ways to Look at Winston Churchill*, she wrote, "It was his absolute faith in his great destiny that allowed him to persevere against setbacks that would have defeated most people."[5]

That faith would now be tested in the crucible of war.

5

FIGHTING AND WRITING

I n the summer of 1897, in the middle of his season of siesta study breaks, Churchill went home to England for a visit. This was the year of Queen Victoria's diamond jubilee celebrating sixty years on the throne. In the midst of all the ceremonies and special events—the length of her reign remains unequalled in Britain—there were naysayers who warned that the Empire had peaked and was on its way down. While it may be that British influence in world affairs was near its height, the Empire still had a span of growth ahead.

It was an ideal time for Winston Churchill to step onto the public stage, and he made his first political speech in the resort town of Bath on July 26. His was an enthusiastic address celebrating England's historic power and asserting that as a world leader she was stronger and more influential than ever; and that the Empire's greatest days were yet to come. Dressed in a perfectly tailored summer suit, he stood just under five feet eight, slender, with fine sandy reddish hair. Though his trouble pronouncing the letter *s* never completely disappeared, he was learning to control it speaking in public so that his audience scarcely noticed. What they did notice was the uncommon presence, resonance, power, and expressiveness in his voice—a powerful sound from so slight a frame. In closing, he declared:

> There are not wanting those who say that in this Jubilee year our Empire has reached the height of its glory and power, and that now we shall begin to decline, as Babylon, Carthage, Rome declined. Do not believe these croakers but give the lie to their dismal croaking by showing by our actions that the vigour and vitality of our race is unimpaired and that our determination is to uphold the Empire that we have inherited from our fathers as Englishmen—[here he was interrupted by cheers]—that our flag shall fly high upon the sea, our voice be heard in the councils of Europe, our Sovereign supported by the love of her subjects, then shall we continue to pursue that course marked out for us by an all-wise hand and carry out our mission of bearing peace, civilization and good government to the uttermost ends of the earth.[1]

The newspaper reported loud cheers again at the finish.

To a remarkable degree, this first speech set the template for many of the thousands that followed: grounded in a romanticized version of history, awash in patriotism, resolute and unflinching in its convictions, secure in its assertion that Britain and Western civilization were uniquely gifted and equipped to lead the world and that the world would be the better for it, and confident that some indistinct destiny, God, or in this case "an all-wise hand," was keeping watch over their island kingdom and its dominions beyond the seas.

During this time, Churchill would return occasionally to considering the nature of that all-wise hand. His reading in India had introduced him to existentialism, but the more he knew about it, the less sense it made to him: "Some of my cousins who had the great advantage of University education used to tease me with arguments to prove that nothing had any existence except what we think of it. The whole creation is but a dream; all phenomena are imaginary. You create your own universe as you go along. . . . When you leave off dreaming, the universe ceases to exist. These amusing mental acrobatics are all right to play with. They are perfectly harmless and perfectly useless."[2]

Common sense told him there was more to the world than what he could see or experience. "We look up in the sky and see the sun," he explained. "Our eyes are dazzled and our senses record the fact. So here is this great sun standing apparently on no better foundation than our physical senses. But happily there is a method, apart altogether from our physical senses, of testing the reality of the sun. It is by mathematics."[3] Astronomers can predict an eclipse and the motion of the sun using mathematics. The visible movement of the sun bears out their results gained by completely independent means. "So here you have the evidence of the senses reinforced by the entirely separate evidence of a vast independent process of mathematical reasoning." He ended with his conviction "that the sun is real, and also that it is hot—in fact as hot as Hell, and that if the metaphysicians doubt it they should go there and see."[4]

While he was still in England, Churchill heard that General

Sir Bindon Blood, who'd commanded many years in colonial Africa and the Middle East, was planning an expedition in northwestern India along the border with Afghanistan. Pashtun tribesmen in these frontier areas had repeatedly attacked Indian villages, and General Blood would lead a putative action to avenge these raids and put the Pashtuns permanently out of commission. Churchill asked the general for permission to join in the fighting, then left for India without waiting for an answer. Blood cabled back that there was no room for him as a soldier, but he could try for an assignment as a correspondent.

Swinging into action with the proven plan that got him to Cuba, Churchill traded on his father's memory and his mother's connections to get not one but two papers to pay for his dispatches from the front, secured a leave of absence from his commander in Bangalore, and joined the Malakand Field Force, a large military unit combining British and native Indian regiments in the northwest frontier.

"The Pathans are strange people," Churchill wrote. "They have all sorts of horrible customs and frightful revenges.... Every man is a warrior, a politician and a theologian. They observed an ancient and elaborate code of honour. A man who knew it and observed it faultlessly might pass unarmed from one end of the frontier to another. The slightest technical slip would, however, be fatal."[5]

On September 17, 1897, Churchill went with an advance team up a valley in Pashtun territory, riding a horse whose previous owner had recently been killed in the fighting. He dismounted and joined a company pushing toward a Pashtun village. As the skirmish continued, Churchill realized he and the others had gone well ahead of the main column and risked being overwhelmed. The Pashtuns attacked, and the Malakans had to retreat in order to regroup and wait for reinforcements. When the British adjutant was wounded, Winston went back to rescue him, but the officer was killed before Winston could reach him. Later, after victory was certain, the British and Indians went back to rescue any survivors. Pashtuns were infamous for torturing and killing their wounded enemy; sometimes the women came onto the field after the battle and hacked them to pieces while they were still alive.

Eventually reinforcements arrived, the Malakans were successful in their action, and the Pashtuns were punished enough to keep the border quiet for decades. (Though more than a century later, the same place, now the Pakistan-Afghanistan border, was engulfed in the same bloody warfare.) His vanguard force could easily have been surrounded and killed, but Churchill had no doubt he would be spared. As he wrote his mother on one occasion, "I am so conceited I do not believe the Gods would create so potent a being as myself for so prosaic an ending."[6]

Both Churchill the soldier and Churchill the correspondent condemned the Pashtuns as savage animals and their sinister religion, Islam, as the source and inspiration for their evil. In his first published book, *The Story of the Malakand Field Force*, written the following year, he wrote of the enemy tribesmen, "The strong aboriginal propensity to kill, inherent in all human beings, has in these valleys been preserved in unexampled strength and vigour. That religion, which above all others was founded and propagated by the sword—the tenets and principles of which are instinct with incentives to slaughter and which in three continents has produced fighting breeds of men—stimulates a wild and merciless fanaticism."[7]

This same merciless fanaticism had laid the groundwork more than a decade earlier for Winston Churchill's next military adventure. In the 1870s, General Charles George Gordon led both British and Egyptian forces in the Sudan, which Egypt ruled under British oversight. But by late 1883 the government of British prime minister William Gladstone, a reluctant imperialist, decided to abandon Sudan. Previous British policy had been to hold on to the region as a bridge between the empire's area of influence in Egypt and her existing colonies in Uganda and Kenya. General Gordon was ordered to Khartoum, the capital of Sudan, to plan how best to get the thousands of Egyptian soldiers and civilian families out of the country safely as the Sudanese applied increasing pressure.

Gordon decided once he got there that he should defend Khartoum rather than abandon it, but the British government refused to support him in the change of policy. The city was besieged in March yet it was August before the government reversed itself and decided to help Gordon after all. By the time relief forces were approved, transported, and in place, it was January 1885 and too late. The city was rescued two days after Gordon was murdered. One of the Sudanese soldiers, led by a Muslim fanatic named Mahdi Muhammad Ahmad, cut off Gordon's head and displayed it on a pike.

As well as being a renowned soldier and statesman, Gordon was also an evangelical Christian who preached, visited the old and sick, and supported charities for children. Not only had he become a military hero in the eyes of his countrymen; he was a

Christian martyr. With the conservative, titled, empire-minded Lord Salisbury replacing Gladstone as prime minister in June, there was fresh interest in renewing Britain's claim to the upper Nile Valley and avenging General Gordon's barbaric mutilation.

To get to Sudan, Winston had to have permission from the expedition commander, General Sir Herbert Kitchener. Unfortunately for the young officer, Kitchener had read *The Story of the Malakand Field Force* and considered its author a self-serving gadfly out to puff up his own exploits. The general turned him down. Winston made the rounds of his influential friends, but this time seemed out of luck. Churchill's big break came when Lord Salisbury read his book, liked it, and asked if there was anything he could do for him. The prime minister wrote a letter to his agent in Cairo on Churchill's behalf that coincided with the unexpected death of one of Kitchener's regimental officers. When the agent suggested Churchill as a replacement, Kitchener gave in. This time Winston didn't even bother to tell his commander in Bangalore he was going to Africa.

After a long voyage up the Nile and a march across the desert, Winston arrived at Omdurman, three miles from Khartoum. It would be a huge clash: a line of battle five miles long with forty thousand Sudanese led by the Mahdi's successor, known as the Khalifa, against twenty-six thousand British and Egyptian troops. This Khalifa, a title meaning "successor" or "substitute" and implying authority from Allah, was a Muslim teacher who proclaimed himself messiah in 1881 and was leading rebellions against Egyptian authorities at the head of a band of followers called dervishes, meaning "poor beggars."

The night before the attack, Winston wrote his mother. If

he died fighting, he said, she should comfort herself with the "consolations of philosophy and reflect the utter insignificance of all human beings." He added, "I do not accept the Christian or any other form of religious belief." Yet he also encouraged her with comforting references to his indistinct but tenable faith in something, the "faith—in what, I do not know—that I shall not be hurt."[8] Destiny, fate, history, something was preserving him for great things, and he would therefore come through the battle safely just as he had in Afghanistan. What that force was exactly wasn't important; he would not sweat the details.

The battle of Omdurman unfolded in the best Hollywood fashion, truth more compelling, deadly, and exciting than fiction. The dervishes made a massed attack early on the morning of September 2. From his position, Churchill saw them "advancing fast. A tide is coming in. But what is this sound which we hear: a deadened roar coming up to us in waves? They are cheering for God, his Prophet, and his holy Khalifa. They think they are going to win. We shall see about that presently. We see for ourselves what the Crusaders saw. We must see more of it. . . . The enemy come on like the sea. A crackle of musketry breaks out on our front and to our left. Dust spurts rise among the sandhills. This is no place for Christians."[9]

Within hours the dervishes had fallen back after taking huge losses from British infantry and artillery that included twenty machine guns. Kitchener didn't want to risk the enemy disappearing into the streets of Khartoum and re-forming for another attack, and so sent a cavalry detachment after about three thousand of the enemy still in the field.

The British and Egyptians charged—one of the last cavalry

charges in the history of warfare—but galloped for the dervishes without seeing a dry streambed running between them and their objective, which slowed the horses and concealed many more Sudanese. Here Winston's bad shoulder may have saved his life: hard luck turned into good luck, just as he said. Knowing he couldn't manage a sword on horseback, he had carried his own Mauser pistol into battle and now unholstered it to dramatic effect. Again outrunning the main body of the attack, he killed, by his own account, "3 for certain—2 doubtful—one very doubtful.

"In one respect," Churchill noted philosophically, "a cavalry charge is very like ordinary life. So long as you are all right, firmly in your saddle, your horse in hand, and well armed, lots of enemies will give you a wide berth. But as soon as you have lost a stirrup, have a rein cut, have dropped your weapon, are wounded, or your horse is wounded, then is the moment when from all quarters enemies rush upon you."[10]

Despite their smaller numbers and unfamiliarity with the terrain, the British and Egyptians carried the day easily, annihilating the dervishes, reestablishing British dominance in the area, and giving the memory of General Gordon its due. The Mahdi, the leader who had defeated Gordon and been held responsible for the indignities afterward, was buried in what Churchill called an "elaborate mausoleum, a conspicuous landmark set on the riverbank" near the battlefield. The tomb had already been shelled by gunboats on the Nile that had "blown large holes in its beehive-shaped dome."[11] On General Kitchener's orders, the Mahdi's body, buried under a slab of stone behind a wrought-iron screen, was exhumed, the head cut off, and the body tossed into the Nile. Kitchener proposed to have a drinking flagon made from the skull, but no less than Queen Victoria got wind of the idea and wrote the general a letter opposing it. In the end, he supposedly returned the head to the Sudanese, packed in a can of kerosene.

For all his appreciation of history and his love of war, defiling the Mahdi's grave and turning his skull into a tankard was too much even for Churchill. Not long before, he had written his mother that he didn't believe in Christianity. Now he seemed to take the opposite viewpoint. Kitchener's behavior was, he wrote her, a "wicked act of which the true Christian, no less than the philosopher, musts express his abhorrence." Nonetheless, he continued, "it is perhaps understandable that it should be demonstrated with brutal finality that the Mahdi's cause was lost and that his cult would no longer be allowed to threaten the peace of the region."[12]

Churchill's official army position was still with the 4th Hussars in Bangalore, where the British officers' chief interests remained reading, drinking, gambling, and polo. During his months of inactivity in 1896–97, when he had done so much studying, Churchill had also become a passionate and expert polo player in spite of his shoulder. He bound his upper arm to his torso with a leather strap and used his lower arm to wield the mallet. After returning to India, Winston stayed in his regiment long enough to play on the first and only all-India winning team ever fielded by the cavalry. He was afraid his disability might hold his teammates back, but the team captain convinced him his strategizing and agility would make up for any clumsiness in hitting the ball. Churchill played, scored, and helped lead the 4th Hussars to victory.

Had he not had polo to look forward to, he would have probably resigned his commission earlier than he did. As it was, he had practiced for months on end, loved the game, and wanted to be a part of the tournament badly enough to postpone resigning until it was over. When the competition ended, Churchill left the cavalry.

Back in London he thought briefly about going to college at Oxford, but was in too much of a hurry now to slow down for that. As he admitted, "I could not contemplate toiling at Greek irregular verbs after having commanded British regular troops."[13] He also had his first experience in politics, a step he'd been planning at least since he visited the speech therapist at Harrow, by running for a seat in the House of Commons representing the mill town of Oldham in Lancashire. The young candidate made a credible showing but lost, possibly in part because he was a blue-blood conservative running in a working-class constituency. He campaigned, he said, in favor of "the virtues of the Government, the existing system of society, the Established Church and the unity of the Empire."[14] But he was beaten by a socialist.

Encouraged by the notoriety and the income his first book had produced, he dove in to write some more. Like *The Malakand Field Force*, his next effort, *The River War*, was a romanticized, subjective view of his war experiences. He wrote about the Sudan, the charge at Omdurman, the frantic, kinetic world of the battlefield. In these two books he was finding his writer's and his historian's voice. He tended to be loose and careless with the facts, unapologetically inserted his editorial opinions, and reflected a very high opinion of his own abilities, position, and level of involvement. The truth was exciting and impressive enough; still Winston couldn't help adding a touch of flash and dash here and there. He also had his way in print with General Kitchener, whom he knew didn't like him, and who got scant credit for the military victory he produced.

The young author took moments for reflection in his work, and in these we catch short glimpses into his deeper thoughts. When he had written his mother about the possibility he could die in combat, he told her that in effect it didn't matter. He revisited that perspective in *The River War*, showing impressive perception and skill of expression for a young man just turning twenty-five:

> I suppose, when we are ourselves overtaken by death, the sur-roundings of home and friends will not make much appreciable difference. To struggle and choke in the hushed and darkened room of a London house, while, without, the great metropolis is planning and contriving—while the special editions report the progress of the latest European crisis, and all the world is full of the business of the morrow—will not seem less unsatisfactory than, when filled with fierce yet generous emotions, to die in the sunshine and be spaded under before the night.[15]

As he was putting the finishing touches on his manuscript, Churchill heard of yet another conflict in Africa that perked up his ears, yet another volatile cocktail of history, tradition, and national pride that pointed toward adventure.

For many years Dutch settlers called Boers had lived peace-ably next to the British in South Africa. The Boers were there first, the British eventually outnumbered them, but the two coexisted as mutually respectful neighbors. There had been ter-ritorial wars, but nothing lengthy or causing too much residual bitterness. Then in the 1890s word spread that there were huge deposits of gold in the Dutch territory of Transvaal. The city of Johannesburg, South Africa, filled up with British fortune seekers who the Boers feared would take over the political and social institutions and, eventually, their gold-rich land.

After a series of political and military dustups, the resolute but hopelessly outnumbered Boers attacked the British. Against all odds the Dutch made significant inroads and put the British on the defensive in several hot spots.

It was just the kind of excitement Winston Churchill found irresistible. Hurriedly completing his manuscript, he set off in search of a way to get to the scene and a newspaper to pay the bills.

6

FROM PRISON TO
PARLIAMENT

ree of any official military responsibilities this time around, Churchill became a full-time war correspondent in high style. He negotiated an assignment with the *Morning Post* at the unheard-of salary of £250 a month (worth $20,000 today) plus first-class expenses paid. And his timing couldn't have been better: three days before he sailed from England, a Boer ultimatum expired, and the hugely outnumbered but tough and fearless Boers invaded the territory of British Natal.

Soon after he arrived, Captain Aylmer Haldane, a British officer he had known in India, offered him a ride on an improvised armored troop train heading toward Ladysmith, near the border with Boer Transvaal, where the Boers were about to attack. Another reporter had turned down the same offer, saying it was his job to report the news, not make it by getting captured or killed. Characteristically eager to be first on the scene, Churchill accepted.

The train that left Durban heading north on November 15 was a sitting duck, a conventional locomotive and cars with bullet-resistant panels fixed to the sides but still helpless against bombs, artillery, or track blockades. Boers waiting along the right-of-way ambushed them, derailing three cars but leaving the engine in working order. As Captain Heldane organized the soldiers for defense, Churchill climbed aboard the locomotive and helped the engineer uncouple it from the derailed cars to steam ahead for reinforcements. But instead of riding on, Churchill jumped off the engine and ran back to assist Captain Heldane, where he was surrounded and captured.

The Boers took Churchill and other British prisoners to a temporary camp at a school in downtown Pretoria fortified with a corrugated metal fence and ringed with searchlights. Churchill said later he hated his imprisonment more than any other event in his life.

Behind the metal barricade, Churchill kept up a steady stream of correspondence, including a remarkable and wide-ranging letter to his mother's lover, his American friend and host Bourke Cockran. Writing on November 30, 1899, his twenty-fifth birthday, he took a pause from the battle of the Boers to consider the battles of capitalism:

> Merchant princes are all very well, but if I have anything to say about it, their kingdom should not be of this world. The new century will witness the great war for the existence of the Individual.

Up to a certain point combination [of capitalism and trusts] has brought us nothing but good: but it seems to have reached a period when it threatens nothing but evil. I do not want to see men buy cheaper food & better clothes at the price of their manhood. Poor but independent is worth something as a motto.[1]

These thoughts of evil and good led Winston to a deeper consideration of war's effect on his spiritual state: "I think more experience of war would make me religious. The powerlessness of the atom is terribly brought home to me, and from the highest human court of appeals we feel a great desire to apply to yet a higher authority. Philosophy cannot convince the bullet."[2]

Before he had scarcely settled into a routine in Pretoria, the Boers learned who Churchill was—that he was from a prominent family and was there only as a correspondent, not a combatant. They decided to let him go, but Churchill escaped before his captors could release him.

Several of the men, including Captain Heldane, were planning to break out. According to Heldane, Churchill asked to go with them, but the others hesitated. Churchill, they thought, was too argumentative, too interested in his own glory, and not strong and hale enough to keep up with them. In every way he was a liability best left behind. Not surprising, Churchill talked the plotters into including him. As if his fellow prisoners needed any further evidence that he was a first-rate grandstander, Winston wrote a good-bye note to his captors and left it on his pillow.

The night of the escape, Churchill went first, climbing out a bathroom window. Before anyone else got through, the sentries were alerted. Churchill didn't want to go back, and no one else could get out, so he went on alone. With £75 and a stash of chocolate, trapped miles behind enemy lines with no way to call for help, he took a chance and knocked at the door of a house. The resident, a mine superintendent, was the only Englishman for miles. He hid Churchill in a vacant mine for three days, then helped him stow away in a train car loaded with wool headed across the border into Portuguese East Africa. Meanwhile the Boers put up posters offering £25 for the escaped prisoner of war Churchill, dead or alive.

Safely in the Portuguese town of Lourenço Marques, Winston sent a telegram to Durban with the news he'd escaped. By the time he sailed back to Durban on December 23, he was a hero throughout the Empire. The Boers had dealt the British a number of stinging defeats, and Churchill's exciting escape was exactly the positive publicity boost the people craved. A huge crowd welcomed him in front of the Durban town hall. At that moment Churchill could have settled into a role as a popular war correspondent with a magnificent salary. Instead, he asked for a commission. Specifically because of Churchill's previous angling for favors and his self-serving books on Omdurman and the Afghan border, the British war office had ordered that no officer could also be a war correspondent. But, the commanding general there decided, he could join the South African cavalry as an unpaid assistant adjutant. Since as a reporter Churchill already earned in a month what an assistant adjutant earned in a year, he accepted.

Accompanying the cavalry during a skirmish at Dewetsdorp, Churchill found himself in another tight spot, this time more likely to be killed than captured. He was riding with a scouting party that stopped to cut a wire fence. While he was dismounted, his horse spooked and ran off, leaving Churchill on foot as a sudden wave of Boers on horseback thundered toward him. "I turned," he said, "and, for the second time in this war, ran for my life on foot from the Boer marksmen, and I thought to myself, 'Here at last I take it.' Suddenly, as I ran, I saw a scout. He came from the left, across my front; a tall man, with skull and cross-bones badge, and on a pale horse. Death in Revelation, but life to me!"[3] The scout gave Churchill a hand up behind him. Winston reached around to grab a handful of mane to steady himself, and found his fingers covered with blood. The mount was pale because it was shot in the neck. The animal bled to death, but not before it carried the two riders to safety.

Later Churchill had the pleasure of returning to Pretoria with the conquering British forces, back to the school building where he'd been locked up, and helped free the captives still remaining. Leaving Pretoria for Cape Town, Churchill took another armored train that was also attacked. Again he jumped into the thick of the action, commanding the soldiers on board and getting away once more without a scratch.

Throughout his South African adventure, Churchill sent his expensive reports back to the *Morning Post*, unconcerned with what any officials thought of them. One of his dispatches particularly angered Lord Frederick Roberts, the commander-in-chief in South Africa and a devout Christian. Churchill had heard a sermon preached by a military chaplain in the field only days after a major battle, with more bloodshed looming on the near horizon, and considered it inadequate. For all his religious ambivalence, Churchill recognized the power of faith in battle and felt this preacher had squandered an opportunity to inspire the soldiers.

As Churchill reported the scene:

> The men of a whole brigade, expecting to be seriously engaged on the next day or the day after, had gathered for Service in a little grassy valley near the Tugela [a river in Natal] and just out of gunshot of the enemy's lines. At this moment when all hearts, even the most indifferent, were especially apt to receive the consolations of religion, and when a fine appeal might have carried its message to deep and permanent results, we had been treated to a ridiculous discourse on the peculiar and unconvincing tactics by which the Israelites were said to have procured the downfall of the walls of Jericho.
>
> My comment, caustic perhaps, but surely not undeserved, had been: "As I listened to these foolish sentences I thought of the gallant and venerable figure of Father Brindle [a well-known Catholic chaplain and later bishop] in the Omdurman campaign, and wondered whether Rome would again seize the opportunity which Canterbury disdained." These strictures had, it appeared, caused commotion in the Established Church. Great indignation had been expressed.[4]

Reading Churchill's criticism of the army chaplain in the London newspaper, a number of pastors volunteered for immediate service at the front to take up the slack, and were duly sent, indicating that Churchill's criticism pointed out a genuine lack that these brave patriots stepped up to satisfy. Still,

Churchill noted, "the cause remained an offence. Lord Roberts, a deeply religious man, all his life a soldier, felt that the Military Chaplains' Department had suffered unmerited aspersion, and the mere fact that outside assistance had now been proffered only seemed to aggravate the sting."[5]

Another unpopular idea of Churchill's was to rebuild ties with the Boers as soon as possible after the war was over. The public opposed any accommodation of the hardheaded Dutch settlers, particularly since they were still fighting. Also, by some people's reckoning, the Boers had been the ones who started the war. "I earnestly hope and urge that a generous and forgiving policy be followed," Churchill wrote in a dispatch, but the recommendation was "very ill received in England. A vindictive spirit, unhelpful but not unnatural, ruled."[6] He understood the opposing view and acknowledged his own two-sided stance on the question that would hold later both in war and politics: fight with all that's in you while the fight is on, then, when the battle is over, join ranks and work together. "Thus," he explained years afterward, "I have always been against the Pacifists during the quarrel, and against the Jingoes at its close."[7]

In November 1899, when he was still a prisoner locked up in Pretoria, the account of his earlier military adventures in Africa was published. Six months later, in May 1900, his book *London to Ladysmith via Pretoria* about the Boer war, compiled from his newspaper reports, hit the shelves before Churchill returned to England and before the war was even over. In July Churchill sailed home a celebrity, a battlefield veteran whose daring escape as a POW made news around the world, a dashing correspondent, and a commercially successful author. This time when he ran for Parliament, riding a huge wave of notoriety, he won by a narrow margin, political inexperience and blue-blood pedigree notwithstanding.

After his electoral victory in October, Winston made a triumphal lecture tour of Britain, Canada, and the United States, cashing in on his fame and sometimes earning a speaking fee of $1,000 a night. Mark Twain introduced him to an audience in New York as "the hero of five wars, the author of six books, and the future Prime Minister of Great Britain."

Despite the heavy expenses of the tour, Winston netted enough money to live on for years, which fit neatly into his plan to go into politics. His father's debts had swallowed the family inheritance, and members of Parliament were still unpaid. With what he earned between the election in October and the day he took his seat in the House of Commons on February 14, 1900, he could throw all his energy and attention into establishing himself as a politician as he had already as a correspondent and author.

Churchill's maiden speech on February 18 called again for compassion toward the Boers still fighting in the field, adding that "if I were a Boer I hope I should be fighting in the field." This was his gracious nod to a worthy opponent he himself had battled. The Commons booed him for the remark. Unfazed, he encouraged the government to make it "easy for the Boers to surrender, and painful and perilous for them to continue." By the time his speech was over, he had both sides applauding.

Churchill the new MP was known as a gifted, captivating writer but had relatively little experience speaking. Nonetheless, his colleagues in the House declared this one of the most impressive maiden speeches in memory. Now, with the same focus and resolve he'd used as a correspondent, he taught himself the fine points of oratory: writing, rewriting, and largely memorizing speeches, even the seemingly impromptu parts and jokes; improving his diction and continuing to work on softening his lisp; standing and gesturing in a memorable way that reinforced the words. "Of all the talents bestowed upon men," he believed, "none is so precious as the gift of oratory."

He flexed his new oratorical muscle in a series of speeches about military spending. The secretary of state for war wanted money for three new army corps. Churchill thought the funding should go to the navy instead. He declared that one corps was "quite enough to fight savages, and three not enough even to begin to fight Europeans." It was Britain's unchallenged supremacy on the seas that had made her strong and would keep her that way. Furthermore, the nation's strength and position as a leader in world affairs was ultimately upheld and sustained, Churchill believed, by "a moral force—the Divine foundation of earthly power."

Even when criticizing army funding, Churchill appealed to his audience's sense of history and patriotism. Opposing the recommended buildup in ground troops, he thundered, "We shall make a fatal bargain if we allow the moral force which this country had so long exerted to become diminished, or perhaps destroyed, for the sake of costly, trumpery, military playthings on which the Secretary of State for War has set his heart."

The source of that "moral force" seemed to Churchill to be in the fabric of the nation itself, won on its own merit. As historian and biographer John Keegan observed, "Churchill

believed, with fundamental force, in his country's moral eleva-
tion above others, by reason on its electoral form of government
and legal guarantees of the freedom of the individual."

Churchill's early years in government revealed that ideo-
logically he was not in the Conservative Party mainstream. He
gravitated even more toward the political center than his father
had when Lord Randolph promoted what he called "Tory
Democracy," a sort of middle way between causes favoring
common citizens and those that benefited the gentry. Voters
would forget it later, but at the beginning of his political career
Churchill initially came on in strong support of Liberal-leaning
matters such as public assistance for the needy. One of the biggest debates in government at the time was between advocates
of free trade, which generally favored the working classes, and
protectionism, which benefited business owners and inves-
tors by putting tariffs on imported goods. Winston believed
the lower prices that came with free trade would be better for
everybody.

Churchill drifted steadily further from the Conservative
Party line. He associated himself with a group of Tories led by
Lord Hugh Cecil known as "Hughligans" that were generally
conservative but promoted policies that advanced liberal causes,
including free trade and accommodation with the African Boers.
The balance of world power was shifting. After the turn of the
twentieth century, both Germany and the United States surpassed Britain in economic strength. This put more pressure on
the Conservatives to enact protectionist legislation that would,
at least in theory, keep the British economy growing. Churchill
thought the move was not only economically unwise but immoral,

and that it would pull down the "old Conservative Party with its religious convictions and constitutional principles."

Choosing principles over party, Churchill kept lobbying for free trade, convinced that his oratorical skills would keep his personal political ship afloat. Finally in 1904 Winston "crossed the floor," leaving the Conservatives and joining the Liberal Party. He was rewarded for his move with reelection as a Liberal candidate and a position in the Liberal cabinet. At thirty-one, Churchill became undersecretary for the colonies. It could scarcely have been a better situation for him. The colonial secretary he served, Lord Elgin, was an earl in the House of Lords with little interest in his position, and didn't seem to mind whatever Churchill wanted to do.

The two years Winston spent in his first cabinet office brought him a range of valuable insights and experiences. Churchill still had confidence in his plans for reconciliation with the Boers even though he had been captured and nearly killed fighting against them. As undersecretary for colonial affairs, it was his privilege to grant self-government to the Transvaal and the Orange Free State, the two regions the Boers had established and defended against the British gold seekers and their supporters. In taking this conciliatory action, Churchill said, "The cause of the poor and the weak all over the world will [be] sustained; and everywhere small peoples will get more room to breathe; and everywhere great empires will be encouraged by our example to step forward into the sunshine of a more gentle and more generous age."

It was also during his time as undersecretary, on a trip to the British African colony of Uganda, that Churchill had an encounter with nature he referred to later as a simile for his views comparing predestination with free will. Yes, there was an intellectual disconnect in comparing them, he acknowledged, but he saw no need to explain or conform it.

"I have always loved butterflies," he wrote.

> In Uganda I saw glorious butterflies the color of whose wings changed from the deepest russet brown to the most brilliant blue, according to the angle from which you saw them. . . . The contrast is extreme. You could not conceive colour effects more violently opposed; but it is the same butterfly. The butterfly is the Fact—gleaming, fluttering, settling for an instant with wings fully spread to the sun, then vanishing in the shades of the forest. Whether you believe in Free Will or Predestination, all depends on the slanting glimpse you had of the colour of his wings—which are in fact at least two colours at the same time.[8]

His conclusion was that free will and predestination "are identical."

An undersecretaryship was only the beginning for this constantly moving war veteran, correspondent, author, lecturer, and rising political star. After Lord Randolph died, the government had asked Lady Randolph to return the robes of office her husband had worn as Chancellor of the Exchequer. She refused because she was saving them for her son once he assumed the post. Now that long-cherished goal was coming into sight.

7

THIS DELICIOUS WAR

The same year he became undersecretary, 1906, Churchill published a two-volume biography of his father. Lord Randolph's harsh criticism of his older son and the fact that he coldly ignored him for the most part did nothing to dampen Winston's enthusiasm for his subject. Churchill idolized his father in print as he had in life, recounting his political triumphs, his wildly popular early speeches, and the part he played in the history of the House of Commons and the Conservative Party with his centrist "Tory Democracy." The younger Churchill was out to vindicate his father and burnish his memory.

In *Lord Randolph Churchill*, Winston further refined the approach to history that started with his earlier books (a total of five by this time, including *Savrola*, his only novel, and taking into account his African history was in two separately published volumes) and would continue in his later work. Rather than document his father's life and career accurately, he modified the facts to suit his view of how the story ought to be, softening the harsh aspects of his father's personality and casting every episode in the best possible light. Especially confusing to Lord Randolph's later biographers, Churchill extensively rewrote his father's papers as he quoted from them. Comparing the originals with the quotes in the book, researchers could scarcely tell which original was being cited. President Theodore Roosevelt read the account and deemed it "a clever, tactful and rather cheap and vulgar life of that clever, tactful and rather cheap and vulgar egotist."

Winston was not about to let inconvenient facts or anything else get in the way once he chose a course of action. In a letter to his wife in 1908, Churchill's friend Charles Masterman described how he lay on the bed while Churchill got dressed and

> marched around the room, gesticulating and impetuous, pouring out all his hopes and plans and ambitions. He is full of the poor whom he has just discovered. He thinks he is called by providence to do something for them. "Why have I always been kept safe within a hairsbreadth of death," he asked, "except do to something like this? Sometimes I feel as though I could lift the whole world on my shoulders. . . ."
>
> In nearly every case an *idea* enters his head from outside. It then rolls around the hollow of his brain, collecting strength like a snowball. Then after whirling winds of rhetoric, he becomes convinced that he is *right*; and denounces everyone who criticizes it.[1]

In March 1908 Winston was so late for a dinner party he almost didn't go. His decision to make the effort after all turned out to be a momentous one. He had just come back from a five-month trip to Africa as colonial undersecretary, then been promoted to head his own cabinet ministry as president of the board of trade. His mother had recently remarried, wedding a handsome lover two weeks younger than Winston, an officer in the Scots Guards named George Cornwallis-West. Winston's uncle the Duke of Marlborough had died, making his cousin Charles Richard John Spencer Churchill, known as "Sunny," the ninth duke and head of the family, who gave Jennie Churchill away in marriage. Sunny had married his own American heiress, Consuelo Vanderbilt, whose father, William K. Vanderbilt, son of the famous Commodore, was supposedly the richest man in the world. The wedding dowry included $2.5 million in railroad stock (worth more than $65 million today) with a guaranteed annual income of $30,000 (almost $800,000 now).

Even Winston's younger brother, Jack, was headed for the altar. He had fallen in love with Lady Gwendoline Bertie, daughter of the Earl of Abingdon. When he took her home to meet his family, she became infatuated with Winston and started writing him coquettish letters implying she preferred him to Jack. But while Winston was in Africa as undersecretary, she and Jack rekindled their relationship and were to be married in August.

Having weathered all these weddings and engagements in the family, Churchill was relaxing in the bathtub one afternoon, one of his favorite pastimes, when his personal secretary, Eddie Marsh, came in to remind him he was invited to dinner and was already late. Winston said he was inclined to skip the engagement and stay in, but Eddie insisted he go since the hostess was a friend of his, Lady St. Helier. At the table Winston sat beside Clementine

Hozier, the daughter of one of his mother's best friends. Though they had met four years earlier, they scarcely knew each other. That night Winston felt attracted to the tall, shy, serious young woman and turned on the charm. Maybe he was on the rebound from Lady Gwendoline; maybe it was the soft light of the dining room. Whatever the reason, he pursued her from that evening on with the same single-minded resolve he felt as he went after a military objective or a point in debate.

Miss Hozier's late father, Sir Henry Montagu Hozier, was secretary of the world-famous Lloyds of London insurance firm, and her mother, Lady Blanche, was a daughter of the Earl of Airlie. For most of her life her parents were separated and she grew up in France. Her mother had had a long string of love affairs, and confided to a close friend that Clementine and her older sister, Kitty, were fathered by Captain George "Bay" Middleton, one of the most celebrated riders in Britain. A national champion steeplechase competitor, he was once equerry to the Lord Lieutenant of Ireland and a popular hunting guide for visiting foreign noblewomen. Lady Blanche's confidante, Wilfred Scawen Blunt, observed that it was "much wiser for a woman who has an inferior husband to choose a suitable sire for her children, and both these girls were delightful, refined and superior in every way."

Five months after the dinner party, Churchill proposed in the garden at Blenheim (he was late for their meeting, and his cousin the duke had to roust him out of bed), and the two were married on September 12. After a wedding night at Blenheim and a honeymoon in Venice, they settled into a house in London. Diana, the first of their five children, was born ten months afterward.

David Lloyd George, then Chancellor of the Exchequer, asked Churchill if the newborn was pretty.

"The prettiest child ever seen," Winston answered.

"Like her mother, I suppose," Lloyd George continued.

"No, she's the image of me."

Churchill now had a wife, a family, a promising career, and a reputation as a war correspondent and hero; and in 1910 he accepted the cabinet post of Home Secretary (similar to the U.S. Secretary of the Interior). His new job gave him an eye-opening look at how millions of less-fortunate families lived, and further encouraged the liberalism that had prompted him to change political parties six years earlier. He struggled to find the balance between respect for the law and class and tradition on one hand, and compassion and understanding for the down-trodden on the other. Visiting city slums, he declared them unfit to "breed an imperial race."

Coal miners in South Wales were some of the poorest working citizens in the kingdom who did hard, dangerous work for little pay—just the kind of subject Churchill felt compassion for. But when they went on strike and threatened the public safety, Churchill unapologetically called in the troops. In another incident in the fall of 1911, two police suspects barricaded themselves in a house in the London slums and wounded a constable. Churchill ordered in soldiers on horseback and artillery. When the house caught fire, he ordered firemen to let it burn. News photos show Churchill gleefully directing the assault, standing in the street dressed in formal attire including a top hat. Again his instinct toward compassion was quickly displaced by insistence on order and submission to authority.

As Home Secretary Churchill methodically considered the authorities' responsibility both to punish and to restore:

> The mood and temper of the public in regard to the treatment of crime and criminals is one of the most unfailing tests of the civilization of any country. A calm and dispassionate recognition of the rights of the accused against the State, and even of convicted criminals against the State, a constant heart-searching by all charged with the duty of punishment, a desire and eagerness to rehabilitate in the world of industry all those who have paid their dues in the hard coin of punishment, tireless efforts toward the discovery of curative and regenerative processes, and an unfaltering faith that there is a treasure, if you can only find it, in the heart of every man—these are the symbols which in the treatment of crime and criminals mark and measure the stored-up strength of a nation, and are the sign and proof of the living virtue in it.[2]

In October 1911 Churchill was appointed First Lord of the Admiralty, putting him in charge of all naval operations. He considered it a good sign for the job ahead when Clementine opened the Bible at random to Psalm 107 and read, "They that go down to the sea in ships, that do business in great waters; they have seen the works of the Lord and His wonders in the deep. . . . Then they cried to the Lord in their trouble, and He brought them out of their distresses. . . . He guided them to their desired haven."

The Admiralty position was a far better fit for Winston's interests and abilities than Home Secretary, and he immediately started on a host of technical and tactical improvements.

He modernized the big guns on the warships, and converted the entire British fleet from coal to oil. This dramatically increased the range and efficiency of the vessels but also meant Britain, which had vast coal reserves, would have to find a dependable source of oil. The Middle Eastern company the government bought to fill the need eventually became British Petroleum.

Churchill was prone to occasional depression, and many years later he admitted these were some of the most depressing years of his life. He called the condition his "Black Dog." Some friends and observers thought it accounted for the mood swings they saw. His personality had become overbearing in the extreme. He was always right in his estimation, and flashed anger at any opposition. He bullied men far older and more experienced than he. But then he could suddenly become apologetic and easily wounded by others' remarks. Whenever this dark mood overcame him, the best cure seemed to be a battle of some sort; otherwise the next best solution was an outburst of aggression. As Home Secretary, Churchill had loved commandeering a street fight in his top hat, and he loved dressing down his admirals now.

Senior officers in the British navy came to dread the First Lord's appearance. Once during a meeting, he was interrupted while criticizing someone who insisted that the old way of doing things upheld the great naval traditions.

"Traditions! What traditions?" Churchill roared. "Rum, sodomy, and the lash!" When a senior admiral confronted him about his behavior, Churchill melted under the criticism. But that admiral was soon retired.

The Admiralty position came with superior perquisites that Churchill used to full advantage. He had a magnificent official residence and an army of servants who allowed him to live and entertain in style. He further cultivated his long-established habit of sleeping late, and refined the morning routine he would follow for the rest of his life. After a hearty late breakfast in bed, he had a long leisurely bath, got back in bed wearing his dressing gown, and spent the rest of the morning there reading, writing, and dictating to a secretary sitting beside him. Visitors came and went, and if they appeared before early afternoon, they could expect the First Lord of the Admiralty to receive them propped up in his fanciful bed decorated with gilded dolphins. Growing up, he had been surrounded by family who lived beyond their means, and Winston, too, tended to spend more than he had. Now he could revel in luxury like a potentate, all at taxpayer expense. An observer at the time described Churchill as "ill-mannered, boastful, unprincipled, without any redeeming qualities except his amazing ability and industry."

Even more spectacular than the house was the First Lord's private yacht, *Enchantress*, a ship of state reserved for his exclusive use. It was 320 feet long, powered by the latest steam turbines, and armed with three three-pound guns. Launched by Harland and Wolff in Belfast, one of the world's foremost builders of passenger liners, *Enchantress* had a graceful clipper bow, wing bridges, and a single large, elegant funnel. Churchill used it for naval inspection tours and also for sightseeing and vacation trips for himself, family, and friends. David Lloyd George and his wife were guests, as well as Prime Minister Herbert Asquith and his wife, Violet. Churchill had no reservations about entertaining lavishly for his own political advantage. Asquith ran the government, and Lloyd George was soon to follow in his place.

Churchill mounted a charm offensive on them and others, even as critical newspaper commentators condemned the extravagance, wondering, "How much coal has been consumed by the *Enchantress* this year? How many lobsters have been eaten? How many magnums of champagne drunk?"

No doubt the numbers were high, but there was another, quieter purpose in Churchill's travels. He believed Germany was preparing for war and was on the lookout for signs of imminent mobilization. In 1911 he assessed the situation and made a remarkably accurate prediction that by the twentieth day following a future German attack on France, "the French armies will have been driven back from the line of the Meuse and will be falling back on Paris and the South. All plans based upon the opposite assumption ask too much of fortune." It would be a bloody, mindless war, he feared. "Democracy is more vindictive than Cabinets," he had warned Parliament years earlier. "The wars of peoples will be more terrible than those of Kings."

Churchill saw tremendous potential in the value of aerial warfare and was extremely interested in the Wright brothers' continuing work. Enthusiastic and determined to learn everything there was to know about airplanes, he took flying lessons and managed to solo, though he was never an accomplished pilot and didn't keep up his training. In 1913 his instructor died in a plane crash shortly before the man was to be married. Churchill's touching note to the flyer's fiancée was worlds apart from the scorching rebuke he'd given his admirals: "May I ask you to accept my deepest sympathy in the blow which has befallen you. To be killed instantly without pain or fear in the necessary service of the country when one is quite happy and life is full of success & hope, cannot be reckoned the worst of fortune. But to some who are left behind the loss is terrible."[3]

Within a year, just as Churchill had feared, Europe was at war. Fortunately, the First Lord had taken valuable steps to make sure England was as ready as possible. In a repeat of his earlier military debate, he fought for more battleships when the government wanted to spend more on the army, relentlessly pursuing his cause. "The Conservatives wanted six [battleships], the Liberals wanted four," he explained; "we compromised on eight." As a result the navy was supplied with battleships boasting the newest oil-fired steam turbines and new, larger guns.

Churchill reveled in warfare. He loved it. It was historic, theatrical, honorable, exciting, and dangerous; and it offered a chance to take part in the great events of the world. The first autumn of the war, he decided to command a reserve British force in Antwerp. After a few days he realized his place was in planning and executing policy back in London, but not before he asked the government if he could resign his cabinet post and be commissioned a major general. Parliament greeted this request with howls of laughter and Winston came home, having gotten his picture in the paper as a field commander dressed in a stupendous gold-trimmed uniform. The prime minister was angry with his impetuous cabinet secretary for sending untrained reserves into combat and presuming to lead them himself, commenting privately that Churchill "would make a drum out of the skin of his own mother in order to sound out his praises."

Even away from the battlefield, Churchill was in his element. "My God, this is living history," he told the prime minister's wife. "Everything we are doing and saying is thrilling—it will be read by a thousand generations, think of that! Why, I would not be out of this glorious delicious war for anything the world could give me." He thought a moment then added, "I say. Don't repeat that word, 'delicious,' but you know what I mean."

Churchill's love of battle, his impetuousness, and his belief he was always right led to a decision that could have destroyed his political career. Lesser men would probably never have survived the criticism and backlash he weathered because of his naval attack on the Dardanelles. This narrow strait on the Aegean Sea, in Turkey near the border with Greece, controls access to the Black Sea. Britain's sometimes-ally Russia was asking for help fighting against Turkey, who had sided with Germany. If Britain could break through the Dardanelles and into the Black Sea, she could bring men and supplies directly to Odessa, Sevastopol, and other south Russian ports, to support an eastern front against the Germans.

The Dardanelles is a tight passage easily defended from land along both sides and from the coastal city of Gallipoli, but Churchill was convinced that British battleships could force their way through. Once he'd convinced himself, he lobbied relentlessly to convince everybody else: politicians, the army, the navy. Against their better judgment, the generals and admirals approved the grandiose plan Churchill threw at them with his trademark bold arguments and dramatic flourishes.

The campaign was a disaster. The navy attacked on February 14, 1915, but retreated under fire from Turkish coastal forts. Four days later they attacked again, resulting in four ships damaged by mines and a second retreat. Convinced now that taking the Dardanelles was strategically vital after all, the army sent troops by sea from Alexandria to land on the Turkish beaches, where, storming ashore in the face of devastating machine-gun fire, they were cut down by the thousands.

The *Morning Post* editorialized that Churchill had gone "from melodrama to megalomania." An investigation concluded that the Dardanelles fiasco wasn't all Churchill's fault; the army, navy, and government all came in for criticism. But his grandstanding ahead of the attack made him the prime public target. Both Conservatives and Liberals insisted he be dismissed, and on May 16 he was relieved as First Lord of the Admiralty and appointed to head the Duchy of Lancaster, a minor cabinet post with no duties of consequence, sometimes reserved as a place to put faithful old politicians out to pasture.

For a while Churchill was shocked into silence. A painter working on Winston's portrait at the time said he arrived for a sitting, spent the whole day in a chair with his head in his hands, and left at four in the afternoon without saying a word. Loss of his post meant losing his house and staff, the dolphin-bedecked bed, and the fabulous *Enchantress*.

Churchill treated his melancholy with another dose of warfare. He resigned from the government and went to Flanders to take what he thought was a general's commission. But because Churchill was associated with the Dardanelles disaster, Prime Minister Asquith dared not spend the political capital it would take to approve so high a rank. Churchill was made a lieutenant colonel in the 6th Royal Scots Fusiliers.

Relishing his role as a commander on the front lines, Colonel Churchill made impromptu grand speeches on a variety of subjects and declared that his first war would be against lice, a constant problem in the trenches. His men were wary of him at first, but soon came to love and appreciate him for his charisma, courage, and unquenchable enthusiasm even in the miserable living conditions of the front.

Life in the trenches meant life in the mud. Digging and bombing had churned up a permanent quagmire that was a breeding ground for disease. Churchill wrote home describing the "filth and rubbish everywhere . . . water and muck on all sides." Half-decomposed bodies washed out of their graves. When he got to France, Churchill was required to leave most of his luggage behind. And yet he was in his element. "I have found happiness and content such as I have not known for many months," he told his wife.

He never complained about the conditions, though he improved them for himself when he could. He got a local tin-smith to make him a tub in order to resume his daily bathing regimen, which he did outside, enjoying his soak while reading pocket Shakespeare and listening to phonograph records. If the Germans happened to be shelling at the time, he wore his helmet in the tub. He also had his wife send him a list of necessities, including brandy, silk underwear, and a stock of his favorite Cuban cigars.

An incident that at first annoyed Churchill actually saved his life, and gave him another moment of reflection on his personal destiny. Settling down in the trenches one rainy night, Colonel Churchill received a message from a general asking to see him. The colonel walked to the appointed spot to wait for a car, but the car never came. Trudging back through the mud and rain, angry at the waste of time and energy, he arrived to see his quarters had been demolished by German shellfire while he was gone. Had he not been on the wasted trip, he would surely have been killed.

In a letter to Clementine he reflected, "Suddenly I felt my irritation against [the General (Churchill does not name him)] pass completely from my mind. All sense of grievance departed in a flash. As I walked to my new abode, I reflected how thoughtful it had been of him to wish to see me again, and to show courtesy to a subordinate, when he had so much responsibility on his shoulders. And then upon these quaint reflections there came the strong sensation that a hand had been stretched out to move me in the nick of time from a fatal spot. But whether it was General's hand or not, I cannot tell."[4]

Was it the hand of fate or of the general? Or the general as an instrument of some greater force? Winston raised the question, then let it pass. But he did add a telling personal encouragement to his wife: "Now see from this how vain it is to worry about things. It is all chance or destiny and our wayward footsteps are best planted without too much calculation. One must yield oneself simply and naturally to the mood of the game and trust in God which is another way of saying the same thing."[5]

God, destiny, something, had already marked him for great things, and he believed there was more to come. "Above all don't be worried about me," he told Clementine. "If my destiny has not been already accomplished I shall be guarded surely."[6] Or as he explained it to Violet Asquith, wife of the prime minister, "We are all worms, but I intend to be a glowworm."[7]

IN AND OUT

Colonel Churchill left the front lines in France in May 1916 and returned to his seat in Parliament, where since being ousted from the Admiralty he had no cabinet appointment and little chance of getting one. Members of his party had been weary of his abrasiveness and self-promotion before the Dardanelles, and that failed campaign made him even more unpopular. Lord Beaverbrook, the Canadian newspaper baron, believed Churchill's "thought turned inward as if he was atomizing his own soul."[1] It wouldn't be like Churchill to spend this time out of the cabinet in too much self-reflection. More likely he was lying low until a new opportunity came along. His glowworm self-image sustained him through a year of relative inaction and lack of influence.

In December 1916 Winston's friend Lloyd George succeeded Asquith as prime minister. One secret to Churchill's political successes despite his personality flaws was that he diligently nurtured his friendships. Another was that he was an endless fountain of ideas, some of which were brilliant enough to offset the inconvenience of having him around. Pamela Plowden, a young flame of his who later married the Earl of Lytton, said it well: "When you meet Winston for the first time you only see his faults—and then you spend the rest of your life discovering his good qualities."

Convinced finally that Churchill's abilities and experience made it worth the risk, Lloyd George appointed him minister of munitions in 1917, unleashing a firestorm of protest from the Conservative opposition. The prime minister sensed it would be a controversial appointment, but still misjudged the intensity of the reaction. "I knew something of the feeling against him among his old Conservative friends," he said, "and that I would run great risks in promoting Churchill to any position in the Ministry; but the insensate fury they displayed surpassed all my apprehension, the distrust and trepidation in concentrated form, with which mediocrity views genius at close quarters. Unfortunately, genius always provides its critics with material for censure—it always has and always will. Churchill is certainly no exception to this rule."[2]

The *Morning Post*, which had paid him so handsomely for his Boer War dispatches, recommended the new minister of munitions be stuffed in an empty sea mine and anchored off the German coast. Another observer asserted that Churchill "handles great subjects in rhythmical language, and becomes quickly enslaved by his own phrases. He deceives himself into the belief that he takes broad views, when his mind is fixed upon one comparatively small aspect of the question." Churchill saw his appointment in a far different light, as he wrote to his secretary Eddie Marsh: "I have fallen back reposefully into the arms of Fate, but with an underlying instinct that all will be well and that my greatest work is at hand."

The Great War cost 947,000 British lives, almost three times the number that would die in World War II. Throughout history battles had been fought between professional soldiers in close quarters according to long-established rules. Now warfare had changed forever, as Churchill eloquently explained:

> War, which used to be cruel and magnificent, has now become cruel and squalid. In fact it has been completely spoilt. It is all the fault of Democracy and Science. From the moment that either of these meddlers and muddlers was allowed to take part in actual fighting, the doom of War was sealed. Instead of a small number of well-trained professionals championing their country's cause with ancient weapons and a beautiful intricacy of archaic manoeuvre, sustained at every moment by the applause of their nation, we now have entire populations, including even women and children, pitted against each other in brutish mutual extermination, and only a set of blear-eyed clerks left to add up the butcher's bill. From the moment Democracy was admitted to, or rather forced itself upon the battlefield, War ceased to be a gentleman's game. To Hell with it! Hence the League of Nations.[3]

His skepticism about democracy in war reinforced a deep-seated belief in a class system that put a small group of elite leaders in charge of the great affairs of men. War had its noble intentions and purposes, but mankind naturally distorted and misused them. In his book *The River War*, Churchill examined this tendency to overdo:

> All great movements, every vigorous impulse that a community may feel, become perverted and distorted as time passes, and the atmosphere of the earth seems fatal to the noble aspirations of its peoples. A wide humanitarian sympathy in a nation easily degenerates into hysteria. A military spirit tends toward brutality. Liberty leads to license, restraint to tyranny. The pride of race is distended to blustering arrogance. The fear of God produces bigotry and superstition. There appear no exceptions to this mournful rule, and the best efforts of men, however glorious their early results, have dismal ending, like plants which shoot and bud and put forth beautiful flowers, and then grow rank and coarse and are withered by the winter.

With the end of hostilities in Europe, Churchill and Britain turned their attention to the civil war raging in Russia. Czar Nicholas, a cousin of King George VII, was assassinated along with the rest of his family, and after a short season of democracy under Alexander Kirinsky, the Communists under Lenin overran the country. It left Churchill wondering, as he would for years to come, whether he had been fighting the right enemy: while the Allies had been battling German aggression, the Bolsheviks had toppled one of the largest and oldest monarchies in the world and replaced it with an ominous new totalitarian regime.

As the bloody civil war played out across Russia, Churchill told a London luncheon audience, "Of all tyrannies in history the Bolshevist tyranny is the worst, the most destructive, and the most degrading. It is sheer humbug to pretend that it is not far worse than German militarism. . . . The atrocities by Lenin and Trotsky are incomparably more hideous, on a larger scale, and more numerous than any for which the Kaiser himself is responsible."[4] Having floundered his reputation trying to help them at the Dardanelles, Churchill now saw the Russians as a menace.

After a brief turn as minister of war and aviation, Churchill was named colonial secretary in 1920. Though the choice of posts was likely for political reasons on Asquith's part, this was a responsibility that suited Churchill's interests and abilities as perfectly in peacetime as the Admiralty had during war. He had already seen firsthand the far corners of the Empire—Canada, Egypt, India—and had unbridled confidence in Britain's duty and ability to bring them the benefits of Western civilization.

Churchill appointed T. E. Lawrence, the famed "Lawrence of Arabia," as an advisor to help him deal with the continuing rumble of unrest in the Middle East. This was a bold move in class-obsessed Britain, where Lawrence, though a hero, was a social outcast for embracing the world and lifestyle of Middle Eastern heathens. What Churchill surely saw and admired in Lawrence was his strength, commitment to a cause, and incredible personal courage, a living embodiment of the classical hero in history. Meeting him for the first time in Paris, dressed as an Arab, Churchill wrote, "From amid the flowing draperies his noble features, his perfectly chiseled lips and flashing eyes loaded with fire and comprehension shown forth. He looked what he was, one of Nature's greatest princes."[5]

It may have been on that trip that we have a picturesque description of Churchill the tourist. Between the time he lost his place in the Admiralty and his appointment as munitions secretary, Churchill had taken up painting, which he would turn to for relaxation and stress relief the rest of his life. He was at Luxor, sitting outside painting a picture of the Great Pyramids and smoking a cigar, when a group of off-duty British soldiers happened by. The men didn't disturb him, and he was too engrossed in his painting to notice them. "With his back turned to them," according to one account, "Churchill, now under a green umbrella, looked like an upholstered toad slowly incinerating itself."

Churchill's speeches and decisions during his tour in the colonial office emphasized his reverence for the law, and the tendency to apply it according to his personal code of honor. To take one example, Sekgoma, who claimed to be a tribal chief in the African colony of Bechuanaland, had evidently usurped the rightful chief's position. Based on the report they heard, Parliament assumed the chief should be deported, but Churchill insisted otherwise. "If we are going to take men who have committed no crime, and had no trial, and condemn them to life-long imprisonment and exile in the name of 'State policy' why stop there?" Why, he asked, shouldn't they simply poison such people, since that method was so much easier and cheaper? "If however," he continued, "as I apprehend, Secretary of State would be averse to this procedure, the next best thing is to obey the law, and to act with ordinary morality, however inconvenient."[6]

As colonial secretary, Churchill was in the thick of the discussions over the prospect of forming a Jewish homeland in British-controlled Palestine. The proposal was formalized by the Balfour Declaration in 1917, which expressed the British government's desire to see a "national home for the Jewish people" in Palestine, "it being clearly understood that nothing shall be done which may prejudice the civil and religious rights of existing non-Jewish communities in Palestine."

Churchill knew well the power of religion and its place in the history and government of world affairs, especially in the Middle East. While allowing for the possibility of a designated Jewish region, Churchill made it a point to respond to Arabs who were afraid their civil rights and national identity would be swamped by a flood of Jewish immigrants.

Speaking to a delegation of Muslims in Jerusalem in 1921, he assured them that

> it is manifestly right that the scattered Jews should have a national centre and a national home in which they might be reunited, and where else but in Palestine, with which the Jews for 3,000 years have been intimately and profoundly associated? . . . The Arabs dwelling in Palestine . . . shall not be supplanted nor suffer but they shall share in the benefits and the progress of Zionism. . . . The establishment of a national home does not mean a Jewish Government to dominate the Arabs. Great Britain is the greatest Muslim State in the world, and is well disposed to the Arabs and cherishes their friendship. . . . You need not be alarmed for the future. Great Britain has promised a fair chance for the Zionist movement, but the latter will succeed only on its merits. . . . We cannot tolerate the expropriation of one set of people by another.[7]

Religious extremism was roiling the Middle East while atheism fed anarchy and mass murder in Russia. But probably the issue that took the most of Churchill's time during his years in the colonial office was another social, political, and military conflict with its roots in religion: the Irish question.

The Irish had chafed under English domination for centuries; Irish Catholics and English Protestants had fought off and on since King Henry VIII claimed Ireland for the crown in 1541. In 1801 Ireland became part of the United Kingdom, setting the stage for Irish-English, Catholic-Protestant conflict that continued more or less constantly to one degree or another. Churchill had lived in Ireland as a young boy when his grandfather dealt with the aftermath of insurrections by the Irish Republican Brotherhood and its allies. He had seen soldiers marching, and Mrs. Everest had warned him against those popish extremists. His defection to the Liberal Party was partly on account of their position favoring home rule, meaning some measure of Irish self-government. As a cabinet member before the war, Churchill had sent navy ships to tamp down Irish civil unrest by shelling towns from offshore.

In 1921, after two failed attempts going back thirty-five years, Great Britain and Ireland agreed on terms that allowed Ireland to become a self-governing British Dominion like Australia and Canada at the time. Even so, the Irish fought a civil war between pro-treaty and anti-treaty forces, with the latter demanding full independence. To control the violence of the murderous Irish Republican Army, Churchill formed the Special Emergency Gendarmerie and charged them with helping the overworked and outgunned Royal Irish Constabulatory. He would never stand for a challenge to crown authority, and was determined to give the rebels all they dished out and more. The

Gendarmerie, known as the "black-and-tans" because of their uniforms, gained a reputation for officially condoned brutality.

Churchill was unaffected by accusations that his black-and-tans were nothing but a government-supported goon squad. To quell the rebels, government forces laid parts of the city of Cork to waste. Churchill even proposed air attacks on meetings of the Sinn Fein revolutionaries. He kept up the pressure until he was convinced that his tactics ran the risk of driving Ireland to anarchy. But once persuaded that it was best for the nation, he abandoned his harsh position and supported the Irish Free State.

During negotiations with Irish separatists, Prime Minister Lloyd George called a meeting with Churchill plus Eamon de Valera, Michael Collins, Arthur Griffith, and other Irish leaders. Collins accused Churchill of putting a price on his head, which he had. That might be true, Churchill admitted, but at least it was a good price, then showed him the poster offering £25 for his capture during the Boer War, compared with the £5,000 reward for Collins. All the men had a good laugh about it and continued with their talk. Collins wanted to find a compromise and went back to confer with his leaders. Two days later Collins was murdered by his own men.

An election in Britain was called for November 1922 and Churchill and the Liberal Party were in trouble. The crisis of the Great War was past, the economic picture was good enough that there was no real political ammunition in it, and the Conservatives hadn't won a national election since 1905, so they were due for a victory. Though Churchill looked forward to the contest with his usual relish, the year leading up to it was momentous. In April 1921 his brother-in-law committed suicide. Two months later his mother, still beautiful and active at sixty-seven, died of gangrene poisoning after a fall. Then in August, the youngest of Winston's and Clementine's four children, two-year-old Marigold, died of septicemia. Whatever he felt within, Churchill did not allow grief to alter his plans. Two weeks after she died, he and the family went ahead with a series of visits to various friends and relatives, and Winston took a vacation on his own, away from his wife and remaining children (Diana, born 1909; Randolph, 1911; and Sarah, 1914), to write and paint.

Churchill constantly overspent his income, even though between his official salary as a cabinet member and the generous royalties and fees he earned from writing and speaking, he should have been comfortably well off. His lavish habits—fine food, champagne with every meal, expensive cigars, the best clothing, elegant lodging in fashionable neighborhoods, frequent vacations—constantly worried Clementine, who, though her grandfather was an earl, had grown up in relatively modest circumstances and always thought her husband spent too much. In 1922 a distant relative of Winston's died in a railroad accident and left him a castle in Wales. Churchill sold the castle, and Clementine breathed a sigh of relief that this would give them the financial cushion she always wanted.

Winston had other plans for his unexpected legacy. His circle of friends was populated with wealthy, titled men who had luxurious country homes, and he had always dreamed of joining them with property of his own outside the city. Instead of banking his windfall, Churchill used part of it to buy a country estate called Chartwell, southeast of London. It had a sixteenth-century farmhouse with large Victorian additions. After closing the sale, Churchill set to work with his usual aggressiveness remodeling the house, landscaping the grounds, and adding ponds and a heated swimming pool.

Clementine was opposed to the whole thing not only because of the expense, but because she was expecting the couple's fifth child. She now had to deal with a pregnancy, three other children, and managing the move while her husband was running for reelection. The baby, named Mary, was born in September. A month later, at the height of the campaign season, Churchill had to have his appendix removed.

The voting public railed against the Liberals in general and Churchill in particular. Political opponents brought up the Dardanelles disaster and Churchill's black-and-tan heavy-handedness with Irish rebels. Though he seldom if ever got drunk, Winston did start drinking early and continued doing so all day, and the opposition used that against him, claiming he was an alcoholic. They also reminded his Liberal colleagues that he used to be a Conservative and so was a turncoat on top of everything else.

Clementine campaigned for her husband with a seven-week-old baby in tow. Crowds heckled her, spit at her, and on at least one occasion broke out the windows of her car. Audiences considered Churchill too fond of war, and nobody wanted to think about war ever again. In a letter to Winston, Clementine reported, "The idea against you seems to be that you are a 'War Monger' but I am exhibiting you as a Cherub Peace Maker with fluffy little wings around your chubby face."[8]

Despite all his and his party's efforts, the Liberals went down in defeat in November 1922. An even bigger surprise was that Churchill's own constituents voted him out of office. As he summarized it, "In the twinkling of an eye I found myself without an office, without a seat, without a party and without an appendix." For the first time since 1900 he was not only out of the cabinet but out of Parliament and out of a job. In a reflective mood that month, he said, "What a terrible disappointment the twentieth century has been. In every country we have seen a dissolution, a weakening of those bonds, a challenge to those principles, a decay of faith, an abridgement of hope on which the structure and ultimately the existence of civilized society depends."[9]

Not one to sit around licking his wounds, he left for Cannes on a working vacation to paint and to begin his six-volume history of World War I. The first volume, *The World in Crisis*, became an international best seller. However, former prime minister Arthur Balfour spoke for many who had known the war from the inside when he described the book as "Winston's brilliant autobiography disguised as a history of the universe."[10] Another reviewer wrote, "It is to be regretted that Mr. Churchill's models have not been writers of classical simplicity and severity rather than authors like Carlyle, whose example expands and forces Mr. Churchill's natural abundance and exuberance into still more ample and tropical luxuriance . . . in the panorama thus unfolded the author himself appears, and in almost every scene he is one of the leading figures. We have thus the portrait of the artist, by himself, in many positions."[11]

Many readers agreed that he built up his own story at the expense of others. One of them remarked, "He sits down, like a Caesar, to write a history of the war, as brilliant as it is brazen, and leaves soldiers and statesmen gasping at his boundless effrontery, at a nerve, a cheek, an audacity that reduces them to amazed helplessness."[12]

Then there was this long yet pointed assessment:

Panorama satisfies him. Whenever it is possible to test his knowledge he is not only—if a blunt and discourteous word may be used—ignorant but strangely unaware of his own blindness, and indifferent to it.

The field of knowledge is so vast that no person can possess more than a grain of it; but that possession, if full and firm, is a measure that warns him how much or how little he knows of any matter on which he must think or act. But Mr. Churchill seems devoid of this trained instinct, which very many mediocre men enjoy. He is armed only with a magnificent literary instrument and at times seems satisfied with any random set of facts and ideas out of which he can raise his lofty structure of words.

At no moment has it crossed his mind that further evidence is procurable and further analysis required. The defect is purely intellectual, of course; he is the very reverse of untruthful, and carries candor to the point of imprudence.[13]

Of course Churchill didn't care. He wrote history as he saw and lived it, with himself at the center. His grandiose style was part of what made the story entertaining, and if he didn't get all the facts to suit others, they were welcome to write their own accounts.

With no political office or responsibilities, Churchill turned to his painting and writing, and to the life of a country gentleman whether he could afford it or not.

WILDERNESS YEARS

Clementine Churchill had hoped her husband's forced retirement from politics would turn out differently. With Winston out of Parliament, money in the bank, and her fifth and final child delivered safely, she envisioned a season of relative quiet in the family. Chartwell changed all that. As soon as Winston returned from his Riviera vacation in Cannes, he plunged into a massive and expensive remodeling program. Bulldozers arrived on the scene to dam up the river and terrace the lawn. Churchill demolished earlier renovations on the house and built anew around the original Tudor rooms that included a high-ceilinged, oak-beamed space that became his study. He learned to lay bricks and spent hours at a time over three years building a garden wall.

Rather than saving a nest egg, Churchill spent money faster than ever. He paid £5,000 for the property and £19,000 on changes (equal to more than $1.5 million in all today). The major renovations took a year and a half, during which the family divided its time between their London house and a rented country place near Chartwell. In April 1924, months before an election he hoped would return him to power, Churchill moved into his new home. To escape both the stress of the political campaign and the commotion of relocating her family, Clementine went to visit her mother in France. Winston took the three older children and, along with a gardener and six laborers to haul furniture, settled himself in the home he would occupy for the rest of his life.

Living the life of a country squire required servants, and Churchill surrounded himself with domestic help, further straining the family bankbook. There were maids, footmen, and kitchen staff; a researcher to help with his war memoir and two secretaries who took dictation by the hour in alternating shifts; a personal valet who brought him breakfast in bed, ran his bath, laid out his clothes, and dressed him. He had as many as eighteen household employees at once. It was luxurious, traditional and historic, very British ruling class, and Churchill delighted in it.

During his time out of office, Churchill disagreed with the Liberal Party's increasingly Socialist stance. He had crossed the floor twenty years earlier because he thought the Conservatives were too unyielding on social issues. Now he feared Soviet-style Communism was taking root in Britain through the Liberals. In the election of 1924, Churchill ran as a Constitutionalist instead of a Liberal in a strongly conservative constituency. The incoming Conservative prime minister, Stanley Baldwin, wanted Churchill in his government and so made sure the Conservatives didn't oppose him. Baldwin evidently deduced that, all things considered, it was better having Winston inside his government rather than outside. Assembling his new cabinet, Baldwin asked Neville Chamberlain to be Chancellor of the Exchequer. When Chamberlain turned it down for another cabinet post, Baldwin summoned Churchill to his official residence at 10 Downing Street in London and offered him the job.

Churchill was overjoyed. Not only did it put him back into the center of British politics; he would at long last be assuming the office his father held, wearing the robes of office his mother had faithfully held on to. To him this was a chance to fulfill his long-held dream of lifting the dark cloud Lord Randolph's erratic last years had drawn over his legacy; to purge the feeling that he had never measured up to his father's expectations; and best of all, to have influence once more in the country's affairs both at home and abroad. He had watched his father as chancellor speak in Parliament, and now his own son, Randolph, would watch him.

Once again Churchill had a government salary and an elegant government-supplied house, this time next door to the prime minister. He sold his home on Essex Square and used the money to shore up his baronial lifestyle at Chartwell. It was ironic that Churchill, who never lived within his means and never tried to, was now in charge of the budget for the British Empire. His father didn't remain in office long enough to present a budget to Parliament. Winston presented five in five years, and did so with his trademark wit and flair. Reporting to King George V on Churchill's first budget presentation, the prime minister said his chancellor rose "magnificently to the occasion," displaying "not only consummate ability as a parliamentarian, but also all the versatility of an actor."

Churchill's deeply held fiscal conservatism led him to accept advice that Britain should return to the prewar gold standard, pegging the value of the British pound to the price of gold, which would keep prices and inflation low. Another time it might have worked. In the wake of the war, the national economy was affected by Britain's war debt to the United States—which they had trouble paying because France wasn't paying its war debt to Britain—and by countries raising tariffs on imported goods to protect domestic producers. Britain's gold-based currency made its goods too expensive and priced them out of world markets. Unemployment went up, wages went down, and the labor unions called a crippling national strike. Since the newspapers were on strike along with everything else, Churchill gleefully accepted Baldwin's offer to edit a government-run replacement, the *British Gazette*, which soon had daily circulation of two million.

Meanwhile he kept up his work at Chartwell, adding stables, cottages for estate workers, a fishpond, and more. He invited intelligent and witty friends out for extended stays, long conversations, and one extravagant meal after another, always served with champagne and followed by brandy and port. Churchill's breakfast in bed typically included melon, an omelet or bacon and eggs, then a cutlet or chicken, ending with toast, marmalade, and coffee with cream. Dinner might begin with oysters and a soup or Petite Marmite Savoy (broth cooked in an earthenware pot), or sardines. Next would be a fish course such as fried fillet of sole wrapped in smoked salmon and garnished with scampi. After that, hearty red meat or game—fillet of roast venison with pate de foie gras and truffle sauce, for example. To finish off, a ripe Stilton and vintage port, baked tart or ice cream, served with coffee and brandy. And no matter what he'd eaten for dinner, he had a cup of cold consommé just before bed.

On top of these heavy meals and the champagne and brandy that always went with them, Churchill nursed weak whisky and sodas all day. He called them his "mouthwash"; diluted though they were, they helped paint a picture of Churchill as a boozer and continued to give his political detractors ammunition for their insinuation that he was a drunkard. He did drink heavily during and after meals, but there's no account of him ever being drunk. Along with the drinking all day, Churchill enjoyed his famous cigars—lit with his favorite Canadian matches, and never smoked down more than about halfway. Some accounts have him smoking a dozen or more a day (quite a daunting task, if you've ever tried it), while others place the daily intake at eight or nine.

Embracing rural life, Churchill tried being a gentleman farmer, but his fling at farming was a failure. The cows never earned their keep, the pigs and chickens got sick, and the beautiful swans he bought to decorate the lakes were killed by foxes. None of this dampened Churchill's love of his new home. Everything, though, revolved around him, his opinions, his politics, and his friends. All he talked about, according to some visitors, was himself. Chartwell could be uncomfortable for anyone outside the Churchillian circle of quick minds, clever wits, and influential politicians. Peregrine, Winston's nephew, was unimpressed during his visits as a child. "I found Chartwell living hell," he said later, "disordered, crazy, inconvenient. My uncle was a great man but a frightful bully. So was my cousin Randolph. All those overpowering egos! All that endless talk on politics! After a certain age, I felt the need to get away from all those Churchills. Otherwise they would have squashed me."[1]

Neville Chamberlain, who turned down the Exchequer post that Churchill then won, described him as "a brilliant wayward child who compels admiration but who wears out his guardians with the constant strain he puts on them."[2]

His old friend and political leader Herbert Asquith saw Churchill as a "genius without judgment," who

> sees only one aspect of a situation at a time, and the ardor of his vision exercises a maniacal and perilous spell. His inspirations, which sometimes have a touch of genius, should have been listened to, and then he should have been stood in a corner and forbidden to speak while wiser men examined them and decided. For unless Mr. Churchill is silenced, he will win in a dialectical "war of attrition." He will fight his foes to a standstill. He will wear them down by his tireless attack. . . .
>
> His life is one long speech. He does not talk: he orates.[3]

The performance, Lord Oxford said, started at breakfast and was still going strong at dinner, incorporating a "Napoleonic portentousness that makes his high seriousness tremble on the verge of the comic. He does not want to hear your views. He does not want to disturb the beautiful clarity of his thought by tiresome reminders of the other side. . . . He is not arguing with you: he is telling you."[4]

By the end of the 1920s, Winston Churchill could look back on a long life of accomplishment. He had served under three prime ministers, held seven cabinet posts, become an international figure through his war exploits and best-selling books, had a devoted wife and four healthy children, and lived in a rural paradise he had designed and helped build with his own hands. These successes doubtless inspired him to hope for even more in the future. With another change in government leadership in 1929, Churchill lost his cabinet post, an expected consequence of a Liberal victory, though he held on to his seat in the Commons. What would be a shock was that when Baldwin and the Conservatives came back into power six years later, they wanted nothing to do with their brilliant but high-maintenance colleague. This, Churchill came to believe, was not actually a case of failure but another instance of Providence or fate stepping in and protecting him. "Over me beat unseen wings," he said.

Failing to get a cabinet post in the second Baldwin government, Churchill went on an extended speaking tour of the United States. He used some of the time at sea for a rare season of introspection, a condensed version of his reflective months in India. His old school friend and fellow cabinet member Leo Amery sailed with him. Here was a close confidante Churchill could open up to in a way he did to few others. In his diary Amery wrote about Churchill's continuing thoughts on the Dardanelles campaign that had cost him his place at the Admiralty. Churchill's only consolation for the failure there, Amery wrote, "was that God wished things to be prolonged in order to sicken mankind of war, and that therefore He had interfered with a project that would have brought the war to a speedier conclusion." Churchill also told Amery that evidence of God's existence "was the existence of Lenin and Trotsky, for whom a hell was needed."[5]

For ten years Churchill sat in Parliament without a cabinet post. Though he called them his "wilderness years," he poured his energy into speaking and writing, completing his history of the Great War, an autobiography titled *My Early Life*, and a two-volume biography of his famous ancestor John, first Duke of Marlborough. He had to keep writing because more than ever he was living extravagantly even after the American stock market crash in the fall of 1929. Churchill and Amery were in America on Black Thursday, October 24, the first day of the plunge. Churchill had invested in the U.S. market and suffered steep losses. Never one to second-guess himself, he took his lumps and went on.

Back home at Chartwell, Churchill kept up his habit of writing in bed all morning, while receiving visitors and dictating correspondence in his room. He dressed just in time for lunch and the afternoon session of Parliament. Dinner was the high point of the day, when Churchill typically hosted a room full of friends and political cronies for a meal that lasted two hours or more, finished off with port, brandy, coffee, cigars, and Churchill holding forth on whatever issue held his attention at the moment.

The real work began after his dinner guests left or went to bed. Surrounded by notes and reference books but seldom looking at them, Churchill dictated for hours on end to secretaries who took turns with the shorthand pad, often working until two or three in the morning. He composed his text as he spoke, trying out various versions quietly under his breath before deciding on the final wording, and left it up to his researchers to make sure the facts were accurate, or as accurate as he wanted to be.

He continued with his very personal style of historical writing. His instruction to Maurice Ashley, a graduate student helping him with research, was, "Give me the facts, Ashley, and I will twist them the way I want to suit my argument." Churchill had become something like the writer he himself described years earlier. "Few authors are rich men," he'd said in his twenties. "Few human beings are insensible to the value of money. . . . Hurried style, exaggerated mannerisms and plagiarism replace the old and careful toil." No one ever accused Winston of pla-giarism; he was far too creative and original for that. But now in his fifties he was an author who produced big works with incredible speed trying to keep up with his creditors.

In 1931 he went on another extended speaking tour of North America, accompanied once more by Leo Amery. "Innocent of false modesty," Amery wrote of his old friend, "he felt himself to be a survivor from an age of giants, an old-fashioned 'great man' in a world increasingly shaped by the commonplace."

Facing a hectic schedule, Churchill had only been in New York a few days when he was hit by a car while crossing the street. He'd looked right instead of left as he stepped off the curb, since traffic in England came from that direction. Furthermore, he ignored a red light because he hadn't been watching for it; electric traffic signals hadn't yet come to London. He broke fifteen bones and had to reschedule the first part of his tour. He took the set-back in stride, commenting, "Nature is merciful and does not try her children, man or beast, beyond their compass. It is only where the cruelty of man intervenes that hellish torments appear."[6]

Churchill remained a political outcast throughout the 1930s. One reason was his seeming obsession with the supposed danger of a rebuilding Germany. After the Nazis came to power in 1933, Churchill began warning that the government there was rearming itself in violation of the terms of the World War I armistice. His fellow Conservatives, along with the British public, got tired of his harping on the subject. He argued in favor of ramping up defense spending as Germany spent more, but his government wasn't interested. The early 1930s was a time of worldwide recession, and Parliament felt pressure to keep increasing public assistance to the voters at the expense of military budgets.

Churchill's pro-imperialist stand on India was another political liability. Having served in India, and being immersed in the romantic imperial ideal that bold, powerful, progressive Great Britain would protect India and manage its development into a modern country, he thought the notion of giving it up was outrageous. India had been called the star in the British crown, but the natives were agitating for their freedom, and some in Parliament wanted to give it to them. In Churchill's eyes, India represented British paternal goodwill, its willingness to help a backward people improve in a way they could never do on their own. The United Kingdom was rescuing the Subcontinent from centuries of tyrannical local government and sectarian civil war, and from an oppressive and miserable caste system derived from what Churchill called the "foul race" of Hindus and Hinduism.

In the mid-1930s Churchill wrote a series of profiles of great men who intrigued him. Most of his subjects were contemporary statesmen; one of them was Moses. At first the choice seems surprising. But the Old Testament prophet may have appealed to him because of intriguing parallels with Winston's revered ancestor the first Duke of Marlborough. Churchill could have been describing either of them when he painted the image of "a warrior-king-statesman who, late in life, became the savior of his nation, leading Judeah to greatness in its hour of need." The emphasis in Churchill's article was not on Moses' victories, but on his afflictions as a prophet.

"Every prophet has to come from civilization," Churchill wrote from the heart, "but every prophet has to go to the wilderness. He must have a strong impression of a complex society and all that it has to give, and then he must serve periods of isolation and meditation. This is the process by which psychic dynamite is made." Penned in the middle of his own self-described wilderness years, these words resonated in Churchill with a special urgency.

In choosing Moses to write about, Churchill again highlighted the dynamic tension between seeing himself as a great man preserved and guided by fate or destiny, and feeling some connection, at some level, with a taproot of genuine religious belief. In *Churchill: Man of the Century*, the German historian Christian Graf von Krockow makes an insightful observation that, in von Krockow's view, Churchill "rejected, even despised, all teachings of salvation and redemption, and only took them seriously as forces of destruction and military threats. . . . Beneath this skepticism, however, lies the conviction from the Christian heritage, that in this world salvation cannot be achieved by human endeavour alone."[7] This seasoned historian sees the dual nature of Churchill's religious connections: changeable and relative on the surface, yet seemingly connected to something more permanent.

Such connections allowed Churchill to enjoy all the fun and celebration of Christmas without the bother of its religious trappings. Christmas was a big event at Chartwell, with Churchill serving, of course, as master of the revels. In *The Private Lives of Winston Churchill*, John Pearson, a former assistant, wrote, "As a nonbeliever, wedded as ever to his unshakable routine, Churchill would stay in bed on Christmas morning while Clementine shepherded the children to the morning service at the Westerham parish church." Then there was a celebration at home, where "Winston was the star attraction, telling stories, reciting poems, and singing music hall songs from his college days."[8]

H. G. Wells had said of his friend Winston Churchill, "He is happiest with a battle on his hands." If that was true, then the ten years beginning in 1929 were unhappy years, because Churchill had no battles to fight. He wrote, painted, worked on his brick walls and other projects at Chartwell, and warned time and again of Germany's menacing rearmament. The only battles were some political skirmishes that further widened the rift between him and his party. In 1936 King George V died and his son, who succeeded as King Edward VIII, wanted to marry a twice-divorced American, Wallis Simpson. Convinced of the divine right of kings and determined to see the monarchy continue uninterrupted, Churchill supported Edward's position that he should be able to marry a divorced woman and still be king, which meant being divorced and also head of the Church of England. The prime minister and others believed the king should choose between his throne and his personal happiness, that the king of England could not marry a divorcee. In the end, the king abdicated in favor of his brother Albert, who succeeded as King George VI, and Churchill was again on the losing side.

By 1938 Churchill was so deep in debt he considered renting out Chartwell by the month, and finally in desperation put the estate up for sale. His friend and admirer Sir Henry Strakosch, an Austrian-born Jewish financier who made a fortune in South African gold mining, paid Churchill's debts, enabling him to cancel the sale. Rescued from the brink of financial disaster, he resumed his lavish living as before.

In March of that year, Germany annexed Austria and continued nibbling away at the borders of her neighbors. Churchill renewed his call for rearmament and diligence in military defense. The government wasn't interested in talk of war. On the contrary, Prime Minister Neville Chamberlain, in office since the year before, negotiated what later became known as the Munich Accord, granting Germany the land she wanted and turning a blind eye to other territorial encroachments.

Years earlier Churchill had explained his philosophy of deterrence in a letter to Stanley Baldwin. "Short of being actually conquered, there is no evil worse than submitting to wrong and violence for fear of war. Once you take the position of not being able in any circumstances to defend your rights against the aggression of some particular set of people, there is no end to the demands that will be made or to the humiliations that must be accepted." Stirring as they are, these words are all the more remarkable for being written in 1926, when Churchill was one of the most powerful men in the cabinet, Britain was riding a wave of prosperity, and Germany seemed broken and inert.

By the middle of 1938 the world was a different place. Britain, by Churchill's reckoning, was tenuous and complacent, Germany was aggressively gobbling up new territory without fear of reprisal, and appeasement would lead to disaster. On October 5, Churchill spoke in the House of Commons in the wake of the Munich Accord. Still powerless to influence policy in the cabinet, still shunned by many of his colleagues, he drew on his brilliant mind, unsurpassed oratorical gifts, and nearly forty years of experience in government, imploring his fellow Members to see the danger ahead.

All is over. Silent, mournful, abandoned, broken, Czechoslovakia recedes into the darkness. I have tried my best to urge the maintenance of every bulwark of defense—first the timely creation of a [superior] Air Force; secondly the gathering together of the collective strength of many nations; and thirdly, the making of alliances . . . all within the Covenant [set by the League of Nations]. It has all been in vain. Every position has been successively undermined, and abandoned on specious and plausible excuse. I do not grudge our loyal, brave people . . . the spontaneous outburst of joy and relief when they learned that the hard ordeal would no longer be required of them at the moment. But they should know the truth. They should know that there has been gross neglect and deficiency in our defences; they should know that we have sustained a defeat without war . . . they should know that we have passed an awful milestone in our history, when the whole equilibrium of Europe has been deranged. . . . And do not suppose that this is the end. This is only the first sip, the first foretaste of a bitter cup which will be proffered to us year by year unless by a supreme recovery of moral health and martial vigour, we arise again and take our stand for freedom as in the olden time.

A historic battle was shaping up, and ultimate victory would come only from a foundation of moral right and moral courage. Speaking in Paris in 1936, Churchill had praised the French army but warned that "good defences alone would never enable us by themselves to survive in the modern grim gigantic world. There must be added to those defences the sovereign power of generous motives and of high ideals."

In 1938 Churchill cautioned the British public (again) that all the benefits they enjoyed as a free people could be lost to lethargy, inattention, and squandering historical moral standards for short-term peace and the illusion of safety.

> Are these hopes, are these prospects, are all the secrets which the genius of man has wrested from Nature, to be turned to tyranny, aggression and war only to his own destruction? . . . Never before has the choice of blessings or curses been so plainly, vividly, even brutally offered to mankind. . . . It may be that our Island and all the Commonwealths it has gathered around it may if we are worthy play an important, perhaps even a decisive part in turning the scales of human fortune from bad to good, from fear to confidence, from miseries and crimes immeasurable to blessings and gains abounding. There must be a moral basis for British foreign policy. . . . We must march in the good company of nations and we march under the standards of Law, of Justice and of Freedom.[9]

Churchill wasn't advocating any sort of offensive action or preemptive strike. Then and later, he felt it was a statesman's duty to do everything possible to prevent war. But once war became inevitable, it was then a leader's job to do everything possible to win it. In a speech on January 7, 1939, Churchill summarized his position: "War is horrible, but slavery is worse."

Britain decided to hold the line against German aggression at the Polish border. If the Nazis invaded Poland, England would go to war against the Nazis. On September 1, 1939, Hitler attacked Poland by land, sea, and air. Two days later Britain declared war on Germany, and Winston Churchill's leadership genius suddenly once more outweighed his political liabilities.

10

HIS FINEST HOUR

The day Germany invaded Poland, Winston Churchill was sixty-four years old, already past a British man's average life span in 1939. Had it not been for the Second World War, Churchill would likely have gone down in history as an interesting but relatively minor figure, Chancellor of the Exchequer like his father, descendant of the famous dukes of Marlborough, an effective public speaker and passionate, prolific writer whose histories were beautifully told but fast and loose with the facts.

However, late in the summer of 1939, history rescued Churchill from a footnote role. And whatever was behind it—God, destiny, fate, the all-seeing hand, the unseen wings—proved Churchill was right; he had been preserved and equipped for some great purpose: to lead the British Empire in a life-or-death struggle against the pent-up frustration, prejudice, jingoism, fanaticism, and fearsome military power of the Nazi regime. It seems impossible that anyone else in the world could have been so perfect a match for the challenge. Those who believe in fate or luck will put the credit there; those who believe in God have no doubt Churchill's leadership was divinely ordained and divinely guided. To the end, Churchill himself kept a foot in both camps.

Prime Minister Neville Chamberlain was roundly criticized then and afterward for repeatedly giving up more ground to Hitler as the Nazi juggernaut rolled across Europe. Even as Parliament debated the decision to declare war after Germany invaded Poland, Chamberlain wanted to give Hitler one more chance. What he thought was statesmanship, the world considered waffling. Churchill knew Hitler would see any accommodation from his government as a sign of weakness. He had been railing against the wind for ten years and no one listened. The Polish invasion changed all that. Once they finally saw Hitler's clear objective, government leaders had a radical change of heart.

Two days after German troops entered Poland, Chamberlain appointed Winston Churchill First Lord of the Admiralty, the post he had left under fire in 1915 after the Dardanelles debacle. The past was forgiven, the liabilities overlooked. Churchill had more experience in government than almost any other MP, going back to the reign of Victoria. He was an expert on the German military because he had watched and studied it for years. Perhaps most important, he had his unassailable conviction that history demanded Britain be the victors.

As soon as his appointment was announced, he hurried back to the office he had left almost a quarter century before. Maps he had squirreled away in hidden cabinets were just where he'd left them. From ship to ship around the world the British navy flashed the news: "Winnie's back!"

On September 3, 1939, his first day in office, Churchill spoke in the House of Commons. It was the first of many wartime addresses in which he so eloquently expressed the government's conviction that they were fighting a just war; that while the road would be painful and hard, ultimate victory would be theirs because they were fighting for the right. "This is of the highest moral value—and not only moral value, but practical value," he said, because it was only with everyone's "comradeship and brotherhood" that war could be declared and victory won.

> This moral conviction alone affords that ever-fresh resilience which renews the strength and energy of people in long, doubtful and dark days. Outside, the storms of war may blow and the lands may be lashed with the fury of its gales, but in our own hearts this Sunday morning there is peace. Our hands may be active, but our consciences are at rest. . . . We are fighting to save the whole world from the pestilence of Nazi tyranny and in defense of all that is most sacred to man.[1]

Winning the war was a divine mission. It's noteworthy that here, as throughout the war, Churchill condemned the Nazis and Teutonic militarism, never Germany or the German people.

As the island nation mobilized for war, its military scrambled to build weapons and put men in uniform. Ironically, Churchill himself was responsible in part for Britain's unpreparedness. As war minister and air minister after World War I, he slashed the air force from a planned 154 squadrons to 24. The London *Times* had remarked at the time that Churchill "leaves the body of British flying well-nigh at that last gasp when a military funeral would be all that would be left for it." During his five years as

Chancellor of the Exchequer, ending when he left the cabinet in 1929, he had promoted reducing defense spending and less money for research into developing the tank, a British invention that the Germans eventually perfected.

Over the years, Churchill had gone back and forth between fearing the Nazis and considering them only a nuisance. In 1937, four years after Hitler came to power, Churchill rethought his view on the dictator's potential for trouble. "Three or four years ago I was myself a loud alarmist. . . . In spite of the risks which wait on prophecy, I declare my belief that a major war is not imminent, and I still believe that there is a good chance of no major war taking place in our lifetime."[2] Like statesmen and politicians everywhere at the time, Churchill considered the ravages of Communism as far more dangerous than National Socialism. He admitted, "I will not pretend that, if I had to choose between Communism and Nazism, I would choose Communism."[3]

A year later, as Germany's hunger for land remained unsatisfied, Churchill changed his view; by the time of Munich he considered it a grave mistake. Now he threw himself into the task of giving the navy the support and direction they needed not only to defend the British Isles but to keep shipping lanes open, which was equally crucial for their survival.

Eric Seal, his principal private secretary in 1940, noted:

> The key word in any understanding of Winston Churchill is the simple word "Liberty." Throughout his life, through many changes and vicissitudes, Winston Churchill stood for liberty. He intensely disliked, and reacted violently against, all attempts to regiment and dictate opinion. In this attitude, he

was consistent throughout his political life. He believed pro-
foundly in the freedom of the spirit, and the liberty of man to
work out his own salvation, and to be himself in his own way.[4]

Churchill was never one to gild the lily. The moment hostilities began, he saw that Britain was outmanned, outgunned,
outprovisioned, and outsupplied. He told the truth and his passion and skill with the language made audiences believe it. He
told the people life would be necessarily hard, but that sacrifice
would be rewarded, and they believed it. He told them victory
would ultimately be theirs, and they believed him about that too.
Though Chamberlain was still prime minister, Churchill quickly
became the voice and heart of the war effort.

By the end of 1939 great chunks of Europe had fallen under
Nazi control. On January 20, 1940, Churchill encouraged the
overrun capitals in a radio broadcast: "Let the great cities of
Warsaw, of Prague, of Vienna banish despair even in the midst
of their agony. Their liberation is sure. The day will come when
the joybells will ring again throughout Europe, and when victorious nations, masters not only of their foes but of themselves,
will plan and build in justice, in tradition, and in freedom a house
of many mansions where there will be room for all."[5]

Speaking in Manchester on January 27, he reaffirmed that
"we are sure that in the end right will win, that freedom will not
be trampled down, that a truer progress will open, and a broader
justice will reign." But for this to happen, each citizen must do
his part. "This is no time for ease and comfort. It is a time to
dare and endure. That is why we are rationing ourselves, even
while our resources are expanding. The cost of living must, so

far as possible, be kept down by abundance of simple food and necessaries."[6]

Little more than a week before marching into Poland, Germany had signed a non-aggression pact with Russia. Yet the two countries soon started jockeying for advantage in Scandinavia, especially over the port cities. The Russians took Estonia, Latvia, Lithuania, and Finland. Beginning in early April 1940 Germany went after Denmark and Norway. The Nazis quickly overran Denmark's small force, but Norway held on long enough for Britain to come to their aid. On the sea the Royal Navy made a strong showing, decimating the German fleet near the city of Narvik, an important ice-free port for shipping Swedish iron ore. But the land army bogged down and the Norway campaign dragged on, with army and navy commanders squabbling over tactics and both lacking coordination with the Norwegians.

The frustrating impasse in Norway, rather than appeasement or any other issue, marked the beginning of the end for Neville Chamberlain. The government and the people wanted an explanation for the Norwegian situation, and on May 7 debate on the issue opened in the House of Commons. After two days of raucous discussion, Chamberlain received a vote of no confidence. On May 10 Chamberlain resigned, suggesting to Churchill that Lord Halifax, the foreign secretary, be appointed prime minister. Halifax supported Chamberlain's appeasement policy and had met Hitler several times. Churchill said nothing.

Later that day Chamberlain submitted his resignation formally to King George VI and asked the king who should succeed him. The king said Churchill was the only man for the job and summoned him to Buckingham Palace to command that he form a government. Also on May 10, Germany invaded the Netherlands, Belgium, Luxembourg, and France.

Churchill's bodyguard, detective inspector Walter Thompson, remembered Churchill's return from the palace that afternoon.

> After visiting King George VI he said to me, "You know why I have been to Buckingham Palace, Thompson?" "Yes, sir," I replied, and I congratulated him on his appointment. He looked pleased but was obviously very tense and strained. So I went on: "I am very pleased that at last you have become Prime Minister, sir, but I only wish that the position had come your way in better times, for you have taken on an enormous task." He replied grimly: "God alone knows how great it is. I hope that it is not too late. I am very much afraid it is." It seemed to me that tears came into his eyes as he turned away, muttering something to himself. Then, I thought, he appeared to set his jaw and, with a look of determination, mastered all his emotion.[7]

Churchill finally had the reins in his hands. For years he had watched as Germany edged relentlessly closer to war. For months he had seen his country's unfocused and ineffective response. Now he wrote, "As I went to bed at about 3 a.m., I was conscious of a profound sense of relief. At last I had the authority to give directions over the whole scene. I felt as if I were walking with destiny, and that all my past life had been but a preparation for this hour and for this trial."

The idea of Churchill as prime minister was not immediately popular with everyone. Some of Churchill's political detractors viewed his appointment with "distaste," convinced that the country "had fallen into the hands of an adventurer, brilliant no doubt, and an inspiring orator, but a man whose friends and supporters were unfit to be trusted with the conduct of affairs in a state of supreme emergency." Very soon even his critics were silenced by his energy, focus, and inspiring oratory. In fact, "within a fortnight all was changed."

Three days after the king appointed him prime minister, Winston Churchill made one of the most famous speeches of the century. Like all writers, he borrowed from others; and in this case a key phrase—having nothing to offer but "blood, toil, tears, and sweat"—actually came from a speech by Theodore Roosevelt at the Army War College in 1897 when Roosevelt was assistant secretary of the navy. In his first parliamentary message as prime minister on May 13, 1940, Churchill concluded his remarks with these stirring words:

> I should say to the House [of Commons] as I have said to those who have joined the Government, I have nothing to offer but blood, toil, tears and sweat. We have before us an ordeal of the most grievous kind. We have before us many, many long months of struggle and of suffering. You ask, what is our policy? I will say: It is to wage war, by sea, land and air, and with all our might and with all the strength that God can give us: to wage war against a monstrous tyranny, never surpassed in the dark and lamentable catalogue of human crime. You ask, what is our aim? I can answer in one word: Victory. Victory at all costs; victory in spite of all terror; victory however long and hard the road may be, for without victory there is no survival. . . . But I take up my task with buoyancy and

hope. I feel sure that our cause will not be suffered to fail among men. At this time I feel entitled to claim the aid of all, and I say, "Come, then, let us go forward together with our united strength."[8]

This was the first of three historic speeches Churchill delivered at the beginning of the war. The other two came after early setbacks that had the potential to break the allied spirit and unravel their defense. The last week of May 1940, Allied forces coming to the aid of France had retreated to the coastal city of Dunkirk and had their backs to the North Sea, facing certain annihilation. Though the battle was lost, more than three hundred thousand British and French soldiers were rescued by a flotilla of fishing boats, lifeboats, pleasure craft, and merchant marine ships that sailed from England to evacuate them off the beach.

Acknowledging defeat in a speech on June 4, 1940, Churchill nevertheless ended on a familiar note of high inspiration, spurring his listeners on to fight on bravely, sure of final victory no matter what the challenge or what the cost.

We shall go on to the end, we shall fight in France, we shall fight on the seas and oceans, we shall fight with growing confidence and growing strength in the air, we shall defend our Island, whatever the cost may be, we shall fight on the beaches, we shall fight on the landing grounds, we shall fight in the fields and in the streets, we shall fight in the hills; we shall never surrender, and even if, which I do not for a moment believe, this Island or a large part of it were subjugated and starving, then our empire beyond the seas, armed and guarded by the British Fleet, would carry on the struggle, until, in God's good time, the New World, with all its power and might, steps forth to the rescue and the liberation of the old.[9]

The French held out less than two months. The Nazis occupied Paris on June 14, and three days later the French leadership announced they would ask for an armistice. A dark situation now seemed even more hopeless. Churchill saw the battle ahead as a battle for the future of everything he held sacred. On June 18, 1940, he addressed the country with another stirring, historic assessment and call to arms.

The Battle of France is over. I expect that the Battle of Britain is about to begin. Upon this battle depends the survival of Christian civilization. Upon it depends our own British life, and the long continuity of our institutions and our Empire. The whole fury and might of the enemy must very soon be turned upon us. Hitler knows that he will have to break us in this Island or lose the war. If we can stand up to him, all Europe may be free and the life of the world may move forward into broad, sunlit uplands. But if we fail, then the whole world, including the United States, including all that we have known and cared for, will sink into the abyss of a new Dark Age. Let us therefore brace ourselves to our duties and so bear ourselves that, if the British Empire and its Commonwealth last for a thousand years, men will still say: "This was their finest hour."[10]

As the French moved toward total collapse, Churchill tried

to uplift the people and government of France as he inspired his own. He even proposed combining British and French governments and resources, with citizens of either nation accepted as citizens of both as they joined forces to fight the Germans, but France refused. He asked France to turn captured Nazi pilots over to Britain before the French surrender, but they declined, which meant the English had to shoot the same pilots down again a few months later when they started bombing London.

Most critical to British interests in the short run were French navy ships at the Algerian port of Oran on the Mediterranean. Seeing that France was likely to turn them over to Germany, Churchill demanded one of the following: sail the ships to England before they could fall into German hands; sail them to a distant French colony to get them out of the conflict; or destroy them. When the French refused to take any action, Churchill ordered his air force to bomb the ships and sink them, including two unfinished battleships, on July 4. On July 10 the French-German armistice was concluded and the French government, under Marshal Philippe Pétain, submitted fully to Nazi control.

In September Nazi fliers started bombing London, the industrial center of Coventry, and other targets in the British Isles. The English Channel, which had protected the kingdom from invaders since the dawn of history, was now spanned in a few minutes by state-of-the-art Henkel bombers. A primitive ground-based radar system gave the British some warning, but the German air force, the *Luftwaffe*, countered by flying in low to make detection harder, and by bombing at night and in bad weather, when British pilots couldn't see to intercept them.

Air raids became commonplace. Churchill and his family

had quarters and an office underground. In order to dress quickly when the warning sirens sounded, Churchill designed what he called a "siren suit," a one-piece coverall with a zipper up the front that he could put on in seconds; that and a pair of slippers and he was dressed. His tailor made several in different colors and fabrics. During the day, when coastal air defenses kept the Nazi attack planes away, Churchill toured bombed-out areas of the city, sometimes with his wife beside him, always encouraging, his contagious optimism blossoming in his wake.

By the fall of 1940 tens of thousands of people were homeless, their houses pounded to rubble by night after night of attacks. But there was always hope, always a bright side. In a speech on October 8, 1940, Churchill noted encouragingly that "it would take ten years at the present rate for half the houses in London to be demolished. After that, of course, progress would be much slower. Quite a lot of things are going to happen to Herr Hitler and the Nazi regime before ten years are up. . . . Our qualities and deeds must burn and glow through the gloom of Europe until they become the veritable beacon of its salvation."

Wartime rationing transformed life in Britain, yet there were some preferences and traditions Churchill never personally felt the need to sacrifice. At Buckingham Palace, the king himself made a mark on the royal bathtub showing how deep the water should be: five inches was the standard set in order to conserve hot water. Churchill stuck to his luxurious, deep hot bath as always, frequently adding a second daily scrub after his afternoon nap, filled up to the top with water checked with a bath thermometer to be 98 degrees, then raised to 104 after Churchill got in.

Since he entertained in an official capacity every day, he was exempt from the strict food rationing that was in place, and he tucked into every meal without apology. A typical prime minister breakfast during the war included two eggs, ham, chicken, coffee, toast, butter, marmalade, two mangoes, orange juice—essentially the same as his regular fare for years. He also managed to keep plenty of his favorite Romeo y Julieta brand Cuban cigars and the special Canadian matches he preferred.

Led by fascist Benito Mussolini, Italy joined Germany in the summer of 1940, and on December 23 Churchill broadcast a Christmas message to the beleaguered king of Italy and his people. They were, he said, those "who guard the sacred center of Christendom. . . . Down the ages above all other calls comes the cry that the joint heirs of Latin and Christian civilization must not be ranged against one another in mortal strife."[11]

(There was a time when Churchill had thought better of *Il Duce*. As he had with Hitler, Churchill once saw Mussolini as a preferable alternative to Communism. After Churchill took a trip to Italy, the London *Times* on January 21, 1927, quoted him as saying, "I could not help being charmed as so many other people have been by Signor Mussolini's gentle and simple bearing and by his calm detached poise in spite of so many burdens and dangers. If I had been an Italian I am sure that I should have been whole-heartedly with you from the start to finish in your triumphant struggle against the bestial appetites and passions of Leninism. . . . Italy has . . . provided the necessary antidote to the Russian poison.")

Churchill expanded on the Christian theme a few days into the new year as he appointed Lord Halifax the new British ambassador to the United States. Halifax was a deeply religious

Catholic whom Churchill teasingly referred to in private as "Holy Fox." Announcing his appointment on January 9, 1941, the prime minister said, "It is no exaggeration to say that the future of the whole world and the hopes of a broadening civilization founded upon Christian ethics depend upon the relations between the British Empire or Commonwealth of Nations and the USA. . . . As a man of deep but unparaded and unaffected religious convictions, and as for many years an ardent lover of the chase, he has know how to get the best out of both worlds." The prime minister may well have been drawn to the new ambassador's "deep but unparaded and unaffected religious convictions" as similar to his own subdued expressions of faith.

Britain received crucial war supplies from the United States, and Churchill figured continued American assistance was essential for British survival. He also knew that influential members of Congress had no interest in getting involved in a war across the Atlantic, where there were arguably no direct threats to America, and that they resisted even helping Britain. On February 19, 1941, Churchill broadcast a radio address to the American people and their president. "Put your confidence in us," he asked. "Give us your faith and your blessing, and, under Providence, all will be well. We shall not fail or falter; we shall not weaken or tire. Neither the sudden shock of battle, nor the long-drawn trials of vigilance and exertion will wear us down. Give us the tools, and we will finish the job."[12]

Three months later Churchill gave his last speech in the halls of Westminster, where Parliament had met since the eighteenth century, before it was bombed. Whatever the destruction around him, he never lost his resolve. "When I look back on the perils which have been overcome," he said, "upon the great mountain waves through which the gallant ship has driven, when I remember all that has gone wrong, and remember also all that has gone right, I feel sure we have no need to fear the tempest. Let it roar, and let it rage. We shall come through."[13]

Before the relentless Nazi bombardment ended at the end of October, Buckingham Palace was hit twice. One bomb landed in the courtyard as the king and queen were looking out a window. Had the windows been closed, they would both probably have been blinded by shattering glass; as it was, they were only thrown back by the explosion. St. Paul's Cathedral still stood, scarcely touched by the bombs, its majestic dome—the model for the U.S. Capitol—rising defiantly above the smoke and flames of the city around it. In November Coventry, at the industrial heartland of England ninety-five miles northwest of London, was bombed and St. Michael's Cathedral, a fourteenth-century Gothic masterpiece, was virtually leveled. Only the spire and outer stone walls survived.

Through it all Winston Churchill stood as a symbol of hope and ultimate victory. Short and overweight at five foot eight and two hundred pounds, bald, dressed in pinstripes and a bow tie, he was an unlikely embodiment of the historic, immutable certainty of the future of the British Empire. His V-for-victory sign, big cigar, and ever-present hat (one wag claimed he was the first prime minister to have more hats than his wife) combined with his stirring messages to tell the world this was a land and a people who were unvanquishable. Of those times he said, "It is impossible to quell the inward excitement which comes from a prolonged balancing of terrible things."

VICTORY AND DEFEAT

How did Mr. Churchill dispel the doubts, the fears, the hesitations, and infuse his countrymen with the spirit that is today the wonder of the supporters of Democracy the world over? I think he did it largely by his own unquestioning faith in the greatness of ordinary men. I have heard him state that men can rise to any ordeal, endure untold suffering, endless hardship, even death, if they believe wholeheartedly in their cause. The idea of death and hardship does not dismay Mr. Churchill."[1]

That was the assessment of Phyllis Moir, another of Churchill's many private secretaries, as the war intensified through the spring and summer of 1941. From her perspective, seeing him at close quarters through one long, grueling day after another, Churchill believed not only in himself but in his fellow countrymen to rise to any challenge, though certainly—again—Churchill felt "upon himself the hand of Destiny. . . . This faith in his destiny is happily linked to an infallible flair for the 'right,' even though it might be a spectacular gesture. I cannot help feeling that he has always seen himself as a leading figure in the drama of history."

Moir added, "He is not religious in the sense that a man like Lord Halifax is; he has no natural faith, no instinctive piety. Rather his own successes induce in him a feeling of awe, of reverence and gratitude toward the Providence that has treated him so kindly and guarded him so well."[2]

It was, she thought, a solidly British way of looking at things. "He seems to have a simple, rather typically English belief in God—The God of Rudyard Kipling, the Empire Builders and the country squire. He knows his Bible well and quotes it frequently. But his choice of quotations is character- istic: 'Ask, and it shall be given you, . . . knock, and it shall be opened unto you: . . .' He quotes a God who helps those who help themselves."[3]

Historian John Pearson, another former assistant, took a less-flattering view of Churchill's boundless self-assurance, even comparing the prime minister with his archnemesis across the Channel. In his book *The Private Lives of Winston Churchill* he wrote:

> In a number of respects, Winston Churchill and Adolf Hitler were uncomfortably alike. Both were ruthless men, obsessed with military power and a driving sense of private destiny. Both were self-educated, self-absorbed, intensely nationalis- tic, and powerfully aggressive in the face of opposition. Both, too, were strongly egocentric characters, overwhelming ora- tors, natural actors, and mesmeric talkers more than capable of dominating those who fell under their spell.[4]

Pearson suggested that Churchill "made no bones about the sense of exaltation that swept over him despite the gloom and grimness of the situation" as the war went on. As prime minister he had reached "the position that his father failed to achieve, the culmination of a lifetime's unyielding ambition. As he put it, 'I felt as if I were walking with destiny and that all my past life had been a preparation for this hour and this trial.'"[5]

Pearson identified a "strange philosophy of life" that "this agnostic pessimist," Churchill, had "carefully constructed to convince himself that he was 'chosen' for the exercise of power —the one abiding satisfaction of his driven nature. Natural gambler that he was, he based this belief upon the enormous odds that had always seemed so firmly stacked against him. In the past, whenever he survived a bullet or a bomb, this faith was strengthened. Now that he had also managed to survive the even greater odds of political disaster to be called upon to lead the nation at its greatest crisis, what further proof was needed?"[6]

Field Marshal Sir Bernard Montgomery, one of Churchill's most important and successful military commanders, winner of crucial battlefield victories in North Africa and Italy, saw the same man and the same characteristics in a very different light. Montgomery was the son of a bishop and a veteran of the civil war in Ireland whose cousin was assassinated by the Irish Republican Army. Assessing Churchill and his leadership ability was much simpler for him: "Never has any land found a leader who so matched the hour as did Winston Churchill when he spoke—in words that rang and thundered like the Psalms—we all said 'That is how we shall bear ourselves.'"[7]

Germany consolidated its conquests in Europe and seemed intent on an amphibious attack across the Channel. Instead, on June 22, 1941, Germany turned against her eastern neighbor and invaded Russia despite the two countries' nonaggression pact. In a radio broadcast that day, Churchill announced that Britain was now allied with Russia despite his hatred of the Russian Communist regime. For now, the evil of Nazism was worse.

"We are resolved to destroy Hitler and every vestige of the Nazi regime," Churchill resolutely declared. "From this nothing will turn us—nothing. We will never parley, we will never negotiate with Hitler or any of his gang. We shall fight him by land, we shall fight him by sea, we shall fight him in the air, until with God's help we have rid the earth of his shadow and liberated its people from its yoke. Any man or state who fights on against Nazidom will have our aid." To make sure there was no mistaking his intentions, he added wryly, "If Hitler invaded Hell I would make at least a favorable reference to the Devil in the House of Commons."[8]

He reinforced his convictions in a speech that October at his old alma mater, Harrow, on the outskirts of London. This, he said, was the lesson:

> Never give in, never give in, never, never, never, never—in nothing, great or small, large or petty—never give in except to convictions of honour and good sense. Never yield to force; never yield to the apparently overwhelming night of the enemy. . . . These are not dark days: these are great days—the greatest days our country had ever lived; and we must all thank God that we have been allowed, each of us according to

our stations, to play a part in making these days memorable in the history of our race.[9]

England was now receiving vast amounts of aid from the United States in spite of the noninterventionist who opposed it. Known as Lend Lease, the policy supplied Britain and her allies with ammunition, transport aircraft, trucks, food, and other essential materials. By November 1941 these U.S. contributions were making a tremendous impact on Britain's ability to fight in the present and plan for the future. Officially, the trucks and jeeps came from President Roosevelt and Congress, but Churchill was willing to give God the glory. In a speech on November 10, he concluded that "we may, without exposing ourselves to any charge of complacency, without in the slightest degree relaxing the intensity of our war effort, give thanks to Almighty God for the many wonders which have been wrought in so brief a space of time, and we may derive fresh confidence from all that has happened and bend ourselves to our task with all the force that is in our souls and with every drop of blood that is in our bodies."[10]

On the morning of December 7 the Japanese launched a surprise attack on the U.S. Pacific fleet at Pearl Harbor, Hawaii, and the argument in Congress over how much assistance to give the Allies was instantly meaningless. Tragic as it was, this assault on the American navy relieved Churchill of the worry of how to get still more help from the United States. Churchill sailed to New York and on the day after Christmas addressed a joint session of the American Congress, rousing and inspiring them as he had the British for more than two years already. Fate and God would save them as long as they worked hard to save themselves.

> Sure I am that this day—now—we are the masters of our fate; that the task which has been set us is not above our strength; that its pangs and toils are not beyond our endurance. As long as we have faith in our cause and an unconquerable willpower, salvation will not be denied us. In the words of the Psalmist, "He shall not be afraid of evil tidings; his heart is fixed, trusting in the Lord." Not all the tidings will be evil.[11]

His words recalled the day Churchill and President Roosevelt had met for the first time earlier that summer off the coast of Newfoundland aboard the British battleship *Prince of Wales*. American and British sailors held a joint worship service on board, which Churchill helped plan and where he said he felt great power. "The close-packed ranks of British and American sailors completely intermingled, sharing the same books and joining fervently in the prayers and hymns familiar to both. I chose the hymns myself—'For Those In Peril On The Sea' and 'Onward Christian Soldiers.' We ended with 'O God, Our Help in Ages Past.' Every word seemed to stir the heart. It was a great hour to live."[12]

Churchill carried the thought a step further in a discussion with Roosevelt's advisor Harry Hopkins, a key figure behind Lend Lease and former secretary of commerce. Churchill told him that there was no better pattern for building the future of the world than the teachings of Christ. According to his private secretary John Colville, Churchill suggested to Hopkins that when the war was over, "we should be content to establish a few basic principles: justice, respect for human rights and for the property of other nations; respect also for private property in general so long as its owners were honest and its scope was moderate. We could find nothing better on which to build than the Sermon on the Mount, and the closer we were able to follow it, the more likely we were to succeed in our endeavours."

Winston still had his detractors even when he was invoking divine guidance. On the floor of Parliament at the height of the war Churchill declared, "Two things I put above everything in my life, God and the House of Commons." Sir Stafford Cripps, not an admirer of the prime minister, answered back, "Well, I hope you treat God better than you do the House of Commons."[13] Historian Woodrow Wyatt found truth in Sir Stafford's complaint: "There was something in the criticism that Churchill did not often take the opinion of the House into consideration when executing policy. He paid the House of Commons elaborate respect but little attention. His aim was usually either to control the House for his purposes or to use it as a vehicle for appealing to the nation and the world."

Still in the United States after his joint address to Congress, Churchill endorsed the Atlantic Charter on New Year's Day 1942. The Charter demanded a host of rights for world nations, including the right of self-government and equal economic opportunity. Harry Hopkins pushed to add religious freedom as well. The Soviet ambassador, Livinov, was afraid Stalin would never agree and opposed it, fearing Stalin's reaction. Churchill described Roosevelt's talk with the ambassador. "The President exerted his most fervent efforts to persuade the Soviet ambassador to accept the phrase. The President had a long talk with him about his soul and the dangers of hell-fire. . . . Indeed, I promised Mr. Roosevelt to recommend him for the position of Archbishop of Canterbury if he should lose the next Presidential election. Livinov reported the issue in evident fear and trembling to Stalin, who accepted it as a matter of course."

In the months following the Allied invasion of Europe on D-Day, June 6, 1944, it was clear to Churchill, Roosevelt, and the other Allied leaders that the tide of war had turned and that it was the beginning of the end for the Nazi regime. Looking ahead to the postwar world, Churchill had a realist's eye for the fact that America, not Britain, would stand as the strongest and most influential democracy in world affairs. Even members of the British Commonwealth in the Pacific such as Australia and New Zealand looked now to America for help, instead of the United Kingdom. In a telegram to Roosevelt on November 28, soon after the American president was reelected to a fourth term, Churchill observed that once the war against Germany was won, America "will have the greatest Navy in the world. You will have, I hope, the greatest air force. You will have the greatest trade. You have all the gold. But these things do not oppress my mind with fear because I am sure the American people under your re-acclaimed leadership will not give themselves over to vain-glorious ambitions, and that justice and fair-play will be the lights that guide them." Not power or politics, not military might, but justice and fair play would be the foundation of a peaceful and prosperous world.

When the Allies began planning a meeting at the Russian Black Sea port of Yalta to discuss postwar responsibilities, the initial schedule called for business to be completed in five or six days. Churchill thought there was no way they could create a map of postwar Europe in so short a time. "I do not see any other way of realizing our hopes about World Organization in five or six days," he commented. "Even the Almighty took seven." And seven days it was, from February 4 to February 11. Yalta was the second of three summit meetings of the United States, Britain, and the Soviet Union to discuss the war: the first had been in Tehran in 1943. Photographs of the Big Three, as Churchill, Roosevelt, and Stalin were known, at Yalta show Roosevelt emaciated and drawn, sometimes wrapped in a coat or cape, his eyes ringed by dark circles. Two months later he was dead.

On May 8, 1945, what was left of Nazi Germany agreed to unconditional surrender. When Hitler committed suicide on April 30, there had been scarcely enough gasoline left in Berlin to burn his body as he'd ordered. Churchill addressed the citizens of Great Britain and the world that day, V-E day, with a now-familiar combination of appeals to patriotism, history, and the Creator. "This is your victory!" he shouted to a celebrating crowd in the tens of thousands. "It is the victory of the cause of freedom in every land. In all our long history we have never seen a greater day than this. God bless you all!"[14]

The same day, he spoke in the Commons along the same lines, then solemnly proposed that "this House now do attend at the Church of St. Margaret's, Westminster, to give humble and reverent thanks to Almighty God for our deliverance from the threat of German domination." At that moment, according to Harold Nicholson, then a parliamentary undersecretary, "The motion was carried and the Sergeant at Arms put the mace on his shoulder and, following the Speaker [Churchill], we all strode out."[15]

In July Churchill, Stalin, and the new American president, Harry Truman, met to decide how to lead and rehabilitate postwar Europe. As a courtesy, Churchill invited along Clement Atlee, the leader of the Liberal leadership in the Commons; the wartime coalition government had been dissolved and parliamentary elections were scheduled during the conference. At first Churchill was wary of Truman, but they quickly became friends. Truman was in some ways a better complement to Churchill than his predecessor. The new president and the prime minister were both men of action, not prone to deep rumination about a subject, and neither of them went to college.

At Stalin's insistence, the new Big Three convened in Potsdam, even though the city, a few miles southwest of Berlin, was heavily damaged by fighting. It took more than a thousand railroad cars of food, fuel, lumber, window glass, and other supplies to make the place habitable. Stalin hated traveling, especially by air, and the site was most convenient for him.

Germany's postwar borders were set during the conference, and spheres of influence for the Soviet, American, and British victors established. (France became a party to the occupation later on.) Ironically, Poland was handed over to Soviet control even though it was the promise to defend Poland against the Nazis that triggered Britain's entry into the war in the first place. The conference also drew up terms of surrender for Japan, and President Truman officially informed Churchill and Stalin of America's atomic bomb and their plans to use it on the Japanese. Stalin was furious at Truman for telling Churchill about the bomb first, though in fact Stalin's spies knew about it before Truman did.

The Potsdam Conference ended on August 2; atomic bombs fell on Hiroshima and Nagasaki August 6 and 9, and on August 15 Japan agreed to unconditional surrender.

By that time Winston Churchill, to his amazement, had been voted out as prime minister and Atlee had taken his place.

The election came July 26, in the middle of the conference. Churchill himself was hailed as the savior of the nation, a beloved father figure who'd inspired the embattled kingdom with a will of iron. But as much as they loved him, the people were tired of his party. Voters were in a Liberal mood now that the pressure of wartime was off, and swept the Liberals into office. As Churchill had remarked way back in 1909, democracy was defined as "the occasional necessity of deferring to the opinions of other people."[16]

The war was won, and even without an office to attend to, there were books to write, speeches to make, and traveling to be done. At seventy Churchill was out of a job. But there was still more history to be made, more honors to be bestowed, and he set himself to the task with customary relish. Whether in power or out, he remained ever faithful to the personal motto he had coined earlier, and which he mischievously invoked with the shorthand "KBO." Keep Buggering On.

WELL WORTH MAKING

C hurchill plunged into writing his memoirs of World War II, painting, and traveling. In March 1946 he accepted an invitation to give an address at Westminster College in Fulton, Missouri, President Truman's native state. The presidential connection was part of the reason Churchill was willing to speak at a small mid-America school. Another reason was that at Fulton there was a chapel that had once stood in London. It had fallen into such bad disrepair that the city officials wanted to tear it down, even though it had been designed by Christopher Wren. The college bought the ruin and had it restored on campus; that's where Churchill would speak.

Truman loved traveling by train, and he and Churchill took a two-day trip to Fulton on the presidential railroad car, *Ferdinand Magellan*. Churchill worked on his speech along the way and read it to Truman, who thought it was great. From the train station, Churchill rode with the president to the campus in an open limousine. He put a cigar in his mouth, but the brisk March wind kept blowing out his matches. Turning to the president he said,

"I can't light my cigar in this wind, and I know the people will be expecting it."[1]

The speech would be one of Churchill's most famous. In it he articulated the form and purposes of the United Nations, which had been chartered in October 1945 in San Francisco. He described a new world order that the United States would lead, and warned of the threat to freedom already apparent from the Soviet Union.

"The United States stands at this time at the pinnacle of world power," Churchill stated. "It is a solemn moment for the American Democracy. For with its primacy in power is also joined an awe-inspiring accountability to the future."

Looking forward, he said, the world must make sure that the work of the United Nations is "a true temple of peace in which the shields of many nations can some day be hung up, and not merely cockpit in a Tower of Babel. Before we cast away the solid assurances of national armaments for self-preservation we must be certain that our temple is built, not upon shifting sands or quagmires, but upon the rock."

In the aftermath of so terrible a war, the fear of Communist or neo-Fascist states "might easily have been used to enforce totalitarian systems upon the free democratic world, with consequences appalling to human imagination. God has willed that this shall not be and we have at least a breathing space to set our house in order before this peril has to be encountered."

He warned that countries must work together to build a peaceful world, or else "the Stone Age may return on the gleaming wings of science."

Then came the phrase that for many historians marked the beginning of the Cold War and, though not original (Nazi propaganda minister Joseph Goebbels, among others, had used it before), was closely identified with Churchill from that moment on. "From Stettin in the Baltic to Trieste in the Adriatic, an iron curtain has descended across the Continent. Behind that line lie all the capitals of the ancient states of Central and Eastern Europe ... in what I must call the Soviet sphere. . . . The Communist parties . . . have been raised to pre-eminence and power far beyond their numbers and are seeking everywhere to obtain totalitarian control. . . . The Communist parties or fifth columns constitute a growing challenge and peril to Christian civilization."

He took advantage of the occasion to tell the world "I told you so," though in a far more elegant fashion:

> From what I have seen of our Russian friends and Allies during the war, I am convinced that there is nothing they admire so much as strength, and there is nothing for which they have less respect than for weakness. . . . Last time I saw it all coming and cried aloud to my own fellow-countrymen and to the world, but no one paid any attention. Up till the year 1933 or even 1935, Germany might have been saved from the awful fate which has overtaken her and we might all have been spared the miseries Hitler let loose upon mankind. There never was a war in all history easier to prevent. . . . It could have been prevented in my belief without firing a single shot . . . but no one would listen. . . . We surely must not let that happen again.[2]

When asked later how he would defend before God his agreement to drop the atom bomb, he answered, "I shall defend myself with resolution and with vigour. I shall say to the almighty, why when nations were warring in this way, did You release this dangerous knowledge to mankind? The fault is Yours—not mine!"

Even into very old age Churchill held on to the leadership post of the Conservatives, sorely trying the patience of his faithful second in command, Anthony Eden. He began to look feeble, but his mind was still sharp as ever. When the Conservatives returned to power in 1951, Churchill became prime minister for the second time, in his seventy-seventh year. During a press interview on his seventy-fifth birthday, a reporter wondered if Churchill felt ready to meet his Maker. With a twinkle in his eye he replied, "I am ready to meet my Maker. Whether my Maker is prepared for the great ordeal of meeting me is another matter."

During a trip to America in 1952, the prime minister was asked when he planned to retire. "Not until I am a great deal worse and the Empire a great deal better."[3]

As Churchill took over the government once again, the Korean War, the first war of the atomic age, was under way. Churchill knew the bomb had saved perhaps a million lives by preventing the need for an invasion of Japan, but also that it could usher in what he had called in Fulton "another dark age." He saw a divine hand both in the invention itself and its timing: "This revelation of the secrets of nature, long mercifully withheld from man, should arouse the most solemn reflections in the mind and conscience of every human being capable of comprehension. We must indeed pray that these awful agencies will be made to conduce peace among the nations, and that instead of wreaking measureless havoc upon the entire globe they may become a perennial fountain of world prosperity."[4]

In assessing the potential for worldwide danger from the

Korean conflict, Churchill sounded once again the warning he had given so long and so fruitlessly in the 1930s. During a speech in the House he cautioned, "Appeasement in itself may be good or bad according to the circumstances. Appeasement from weakness and fear is alike futile and fatal. Appeasement from strength is magnanimous and noble, and might be the surest and perhaps the only path to world peace."

Churchill had twice rejected the offer of a peerage during his long career because he thought it would hamper his son's chances in politics. Prime ministers traditionally came from the House of Commons, where members were elected, and not the House of Lords, where the members served as a hereditary right. As a peer, Churchill would have a noble title and a seat in the Lords that would pass to his son upon his death. By accepting the honor, Churchill feared that when he died and the title passed to Randolph it would keep him from the top spot. What Churchill didn't see, but what everyone else who knew him did, was that his son was in no way fit to be prime minister. He had all his father's most undesirable characteristics with none of his offsetting advantages. He was conceited, rude, overbearing, and thoughtless of others. In addition he was a drunkard with no sense of social graces. (Regarding his personal beliefs, Randolph had no room whatsoever for religion. His father's friend, novelist Evelyn Waugh, once bet Randolph ten pounds he couldn't read the Bible all the way through from beginning to end. He made it to the end of the Old Testament before giving up in disgust, complaining to Waugh, "God! Wasn't God a sh—!")[5]

Churchill had never been a family man, and other than his son's frustrated political ambitions, he seemed to not have paid his children much attention, which should be no surprise considering the way he himself was raised and his single-minded immersion in politics. Twice divorced, Randolph would die of a heart attack in 1968. His older sister, Diana, also twice divorced, committed suicide in 1963. The third child, Sarah, married an Austrian-born BBC radio star and became an actress; she was divorced once and widowed twice, and died in 1982. The youngest child, Mary, was the most stable of the lot, and worked for the Red Cross during the war, traveled as an aide-de-camp to her father, and later chaired the Royal National Theater; widowed after forty years of marriage to a baron, she was awarded the Order of the British Empire and, in 2005, a Lady Companion of the Order of the Garter.

In 1953 Churchill was made a Knight Companion of the Order of the Garter, an honor that bestowed upon him the title of Sir Winston, but which was not hereditary. The number of Companions is traditionally limited to twenty-four, and membership is a personal honor given only by the sovereign. Two months later Churchill had a stroke, which he kept secret from all but a handful of insiders; he confided in his friend President Dwight Eisenhower, whom he had come to admire during the war when Eisenhower was supreme allied commander. Writing to the president about his condition, he mentioned President Woodrow Wilson, who was so incapacitated at the end of his presidency that his wife and advisors secretly ran the government on his behalf.

Getting around even more slowly now, the prime minister felt his political colleagues' gently but steadily increasing pressure on him to retire. For all his physical feebleness, he seemed to have lost none of his edge or intellectual spark. The year of his stroke and his Order of the Garter honor, he won the Nobel

Prize in history for his six-volume account of the Second World War. Though the set focused heavily on the fighting in Western Europe at the expense of the Eastern front and the Pacific, it was a runaway best seller. Since he couldn't actually copy or keep government documents for his personal research, he'd had summaries and quotations from them made and sent to Chartwell during the war, giving his story a level of detail other authors could never match. As always, he adjusted the facts to serve his purpose. Coming across undeniable evidence that a story he wanted to use in a later book was false, he complained, "Grouchy old researchers have destroyed this splendid legend, but it should still have its place in any history book worthy of the name." Challenged on a particular point, Churchill declared it was nothing more than a "terminological inexactitude."[6]

In November 1954, shortly before his eightieth birthday, Churchill had another stroke. His time seemed to be growing short, yet he clung to power a little longer. Responding—with a forgivable note of false modesty—to the long recitation of accolades during his eightieth birthday celebration, he said, "I have never accepted what many people have kindly said, namely that I inspired the nation. Their will was resolute and remorseless, and, as it proved, unconquerable. It fell to me to express it, and if I found the right words you must remember that I have always earned my living by my pen and by my tongue. It was the nation and the race dwelling all round the globe that had the lion's heart. I had the luck to be called on to give it the roar."[7]

On the occasion a portrait by Graham Sutherland was unveiled as a gift to Churchill and his wife. Sutherland was a distinguished art professor, painter, stained-glass artist, and tapestry designer who would later contribute some of the decoration for the new Coventry Cathedral. His painting of Sir Winston showed the subject seated in a chair, a hand clutching each armrest, the low angle accentuating the lines and wrinkles of his neck and jaw. In the style of the times, the shadows had a deep greenish cast to them. Though they were gracious and appreciative in public, Winston and Clementine both despised the picture; it was soon destroyed on Clementine's orders.

The night of April 4, 1955, Winston Churchill made history yet again by becoming the first prime minister ever to host the queen for dinner at his official residence, 10 Downing Street in London, rather than dining at the palace. It was a mark of young Elizabeth II's respect for her faithful and long-serving subject, the last active member of Parliament to have served under her great-great-grandmother, Queen Victoria. A photograph shows him escorting the queen and Prince Philip to her Rolls-Royce at the end of the evening, the queen resplendent in an evening gown and tiara, and Churchill in traditional full court dress including knee breeches and shoes with buckles.

The next day he announced his resignation as prime minister. Finally he'd accepted the fact that his age had caught up with him. In an undated letter to President Eisenhower written around April 1, he wrote that it was his duty as leader of his party "to make sure that my successor has a fair chance of leading the Conservatives to victory at the next Election." He feared a Socialist takeover in Britain and believed the Conservative leader would have to be a strong force in the campaign. "This at my age I could not undertake to do," he explained. "Hence I have felt it my duty to resign." However, he added, "To resign is not to retire," and he would keep working for improvement of the "Anglo-American brother-hood" and for "the arrest of the Communist menace."

Though he retained his seat in Parliament, Churchill attended the sessions less and less. He spent the last years of his life paint-ing and writing at Chartwell, visiting the Riviera, and cruising the Mediterranean on yachts of the rich and famous, including Aristotle Onassis. A year after stepping down as prime minis-ter, he published the first of two volumes on *The History of the English-Speaking Peoples*.

In the twilight of life Churchill reflected from time to time on what lay ahead for him. He'd thought and written about the sub-ject for decades. In *Amid These Storms*, a collection of essays from the 1920s, he predicted, "When I get to Heaven I mean to spend a considerable portion of my five million years in painting, and so get to the bottom of the subject. But then I shall require a still gayer palette than I get here below.... There will be a whole range of wonderful new colours which will delight the celestial eye."[8]

Writing in *Thoughts and Adventures* during the difficult years of the 1930s, he confidently suggested that the threaten-ing darkness of the period made the world more grateful for the light: "Let us be contented with what has happened to us and thankful for all we have been spared. Let us accept the natural order in which we move. Let us reconcile ourselves to the mysterious rhythm of our destinies, such as they must be in this world of space and time. Let us treasure our joys but not bewail our sorrows. The glory of light cannot exist without its shadows. Life is a whole, and good and ill must be accepted together. The journey has been enjoyable and well worth making—once."[9]

In the 1940s, after unconditional victory in a devastating world war and learning of the terrible power of atomic weapons, he pondered the afterlife again:

I wonder what God thinks of the things His creatures have invented. Really, it's surprising He has allowed it—but then I suppose he has so many things to think of, not only us, but all His worlds. I wouldn't have His job for anything. Mine is hard enough, but his is much more difficult. And—umph—He can't even resign. . . .

You know, most people are going to be very surprised when they get to Heaven. They are looking forward to meeting fascinating people like Napoleon and Julius Caesar. But they'll probably never even be able to find them, because there will be so many millions of other people there too—Indians and Chinese and people like that. Everyone will have equal rights in Heaven. That will be the real Welfare State.[10]

A reporter asked him what made him so sure he'd make it to heaven. Jovially he replied, "Surely the Almighty must observe the principles of English common law and consider a man innocent until proven guilty." Another time Churchill lightheartedly imagined the afterlife as "some kind of velvety cool blackness. Of course, I admit I may be wrong. It is conceivable that I might well be reborn as a Chinese coolie. In such case I should lodge a protest."[11]

Roy Howells, a private nurse hired to watch over him day and night, wrote of Churchill that near the end, "two things let him down . . . his legs and his hearing. This unfortunately gave people the impression that he was just an old man obstinately clinging to life. . . . But senility, after all, implies a state of feeble-mindedness, and he was never by any stretch of the imagination feeble-minded, even at the end."[12]

He was, however, mercurial as ever when he didn't get his way. Churchill broke his spine in a fall and afterward was supposed to sleep with a bedrest, which he hated. Howells remembered one time when "we had a blazing row over the bedrest and I'm afraid we swore at each other. Afterward we made it up. Sir Winston, his bottom lip jutting, said, 'You were very rude to me, you know.' I told him, 'Yes, but you were rude too.' Then, with just a hint of a smile, he looked up and said blandly, 'Yes, but I *am* a great man.' There was no answer to that. He knew, as I and the rest of the world knew, that he was right."[13]

Howells continued. "Other members of the household saw only the legend; we had to deal with the man. . . . It took me a little while to get used to the fact that in two days his cigar consumption was the equivalent of my weekly salary."[14]

Sir Winston's last appearance at the Commons was on July 27, 1964. Prime Minister Harold Macmillan led the way in showering the old lion with praises. "The life of the man whom we are honoring today is unique," he told the members of the chamber. "The oldest among us can recall nothing to compare with it, and the younger ones among you, however long you live, will never see the like again."[15]

His last international accolade had been an honorary American citizenship awarded by Congress and President John F. Kennedy the year before. He was too frail to accept the honor in person, but watched the ceremony on television live via satellite.

On January 15, 1965, Churchill was felled by another stroke, and the velvety cool blackness started closing in. At the end, nine days later, Clementine stood on one side of his bed and Randolph on the other, the rest of the family close around, with Mary leading the grandchildren in and out for one last visit. Reportedly, his last words were to Mary's husband, Christopher Soames, who had tried to offer him champagne. "I'm so bored with it all."[16] It was seventy years to the day after his father passed away. Winston had long predicted he would die on the anniversary.

For the first time in the twentieth century, the monarch ordered a state funeral for a commoner; Queen Elizabeth attended, the only occasion the British sovereign has ever come to a funeral service for a nonroyal. After lying in state for three days, the coffin was loaded on a gun caisson for the procession to St. Paul's Cathedral. Uniformed troops by the hundreds marched in ranks through the bitter cold of a London winter day. In honor of Churchill's American heritage, the congregation sang the "Battle Hymn of the Republic" during the service. Afterward, Churchill's coffin was loaded onto a launch on the River Thames, then taken to Waterloo Station for the final journey by rail to the parish churchyard of Bladon, where his parents were buried, and in sight of Blenheim, where the whole adventure began.

Later that year, Adlai Stevenson, American ambassador to the UN and former governor of Illinois, wrote in an essay that Churchill's death left "a lonesome place against the sky." He continued,

> There is a feeling that, as Harvard historian H. Stuart Hughes puts it, today's world has "little tolerance of greatness," and that in an era of computers, expert teams and government by

consensus, the Churchillian kind of leadership may never again assert itself. With Churchill's passing, the world was diminished and felt it. Amid all the public outpourings of tribute and grief, however, no words struck a nobler note than the heartsick message that Winston Churchill himself broadcast to the people of defeated France in 1940: "Good night, then: sleep to gather strength for the morning, for the morning will come. Brightly will it shine on the brave and true, the kindly, on all who suffer for the cause, and gloriously upon the tombs of heroes. Thus will shine the dawn."[17]

Since 1981 Westminster College has hosted the Crosby Kemper Lectures, an annual lecture by authorities on Winston Churchill and British history. In 1991 Churchill's youngest daughter, Mary, Lady Soames, gave the lecture and in it summed up her father's outlook:

> What of my father's philosophy of life? He certainly had faith in the indomitable spirit of man. Taking leave of his government ministers in 1955, he used the phrase, "Man is spirit."
>
> But what of his faith in God? Winston Churchill was not religious in a conventional sense—and certainly no regular churchgoer. I saw him once greatly embarrassed when a visiting divine addressed him as a "pillar of the church." My father, one of whose endearing qualities was candor, replied, "Well, I don't think that could be said of me. But I do like to think of myself as a flying buttress."
>
> He had a strong underlying belief in a providential God. When the call to him came in 1940, he later was to write; "I felt as if I were walking with destiny, and that all my past life had

been a preparation for this hour and this trial." And indeed when one looks back upon the hazards and dangers through which he has passed—the illnesses and accidents he suffered in his youth, the numerous close encounters with death in his soldier-of-fortune days—it is hard not to see a guiding and guarding hand, and he himself felt this element increasingly.

On death, I have heard him express different thoughts. The concept of a "deep velvet sleep" at times seemed a pleasing option. But this was among the musings of an old man. To Clementine, in his prime, when life and love and ambition throbbed in his veins, he revealed a belief in which valiant hope and a certain tinge of uncertainty seems to be mingled. In July 1915 he wrote a letter marked "To be sent to Mrs. Churchill in the event of my death": "Do not grieve for me too much. I am a spirit confident of my rights. Death is only an incident, and not the most important which happens to us in this state of being. On the whole, and especially since I met you my darling one, I have been happy, and you have taught me how noble a woman's heart can be. If there is anywhere else, I shall be on the lookout for you."[18]

A valiant hope and a certain tinge of uncertainty—that was Churchill's double-sided view of the world in a nutshell. Sometimes the hope prevailed and at others the uncertainty held sway. But looking over his long and remarkable life, it was the hope that won out; hope that inspired and drove him beyond the petty and selfish and agnostic, beyond the lisp and concussions and mangled shoulder, beyond the Dardanelles and defeats and disappointments, to a hero's end.

NOTES

CHAPTER 1

1. Henrietta Spencer-Churchill, *Blenheim and the Churchill Family: A Personal Portrait* (New York: Rizzoli, 2005), 54.
2. Ibid., 139.
3. Norman Rose, *Churchill: The Unruly Giant* (New York: The Free Press, 1994), 10.
4. Winston S. Churchill, *My Early Life: A Roving Commission* (New York: Charles Scribner's Sons, 1930), 2.
5. Celia Sandys, *The Young Churchill: The Early Years of Winston Churchill* (New York: Dutton, 1994), 33.
6. Churchill, *My Early Life*, 12.

CHAPTER 2

1. Churchill, *My Early Life*, 13.
2. Ibid.
3. Sandys, *The Young Churchill*, 79.
4. Ibid., 124.
5. Ibid., 170.
6. Ibid.
7. Ibid., 142.
8. Ibid., 160.

CHAPTER 3

1. Sandys, *The Young Churchill*, 176.
2. Ibid., 181.
3. Ibid., 210.
4. Ibid.
5. Ibid.
6. Churchill, *My Early Life*, 50.

7. Rose, *Churchill: The Unruly Giant*, 24.
8. Ibid.
9. Ibid.
10. Ibid.
11. Churchill, *My Early Life*, 73.
12. Ibid.

CHAPTER 4

1. Churchill, *My Early Life*, 75.
2. Ibid., 102.
3. Ibid., 109.
4. Ibid., 113.
5. Gretchen Ruben, *Forty Ways to Look at Winston Churchill: A Brief Account of a Long Life* (New York: Ballantine Books, 2003)

CHAPTER 5

1. Winston S. Churchill, *Never Give In! The Best of Winston Churchill's Speeches: Selected by His Grandson* (New York: Hyperion, 2003), 4.
2. Churchill, *My Early Life*, 117.
3. Ibid.
4. Ibid.
5. Ibid., 129.
6. John Pearson, *The Private Lives of Winston Churchill* (New York: Simon & Schuster, 1991), 98.
7. Winston S. Churchill, *The Story of the Malakand Field Force* (n.p.: Seven Treasures Publications, 2009), 30.
8. Churchill, *My Early Life*, 183.
9. Ibid.
10. Ibid.
11. Ibid.
12. Ibid.
13. Ibid., 203.
14. Ibid., 220.
15. Kay Halle, ed., *Irrepressible Churchill: A Treasury of Winston Churchill's Wit* (Cleveland: The World Publishing Company, 1966), 345.
16. Ibid.

Chapter 6

1. Martin Gilbert, *In Search of Churchill: A Historian's Journey* (New York: John Wiley & Sons, Inc., 1994), 278.
2. Ibid.
3. Michael Paterson, *Winston Churchill: Personal Accounts of the Great Leader at War* (Newton Abbot: David and Charles, 2005), 170.
4. Churchill, *My Early Life*, 132.
5. Ibid.
6. Ibid., 329–30.
7. Ibid.
8. Ibid., 28.

Chapter 7

1. John Lukacs, *Man of the Century: A Churchill Cavalcade Compiled by Editors of* The Reader's Digest (Boston: Little, Brown and Company, 1965), 41.
2. Gilbert, *In Search of Churchill*, 269.
3. Ibid., 284.
4. Paterson, *Winston Churchill: Personal Accounts*, 215.
5. Ibid.
6. Ibid.
7. Pearson, *The Private Lives of Winston Churchill*, 175.

Chapter 8

1. Pearson, *The Private Lives of Winston Churchill*, 157.
2. Lukacs, *Man of the Century*, 90.
3. Churchill, *My Early Life*, 65.
4. Churchill, *Never Give In!*, 77.
5. Lukacs, *Man of the Century*, 108.
6. Peter Stansky, ed., *Churchill: A Profile* (New York: Hill and Wang, 1973), 24.
7. Churchill, *Never Give In!*, 79.
8. Rose, *Churchill: The Unruly Giant*, 202.
9. Ibid., 181.
10. Lukacs, *Man of the Century*, 112.

11. Stansky, *Churchill: A Profile*, 39.

12. Ibid.

13. Ibid.

Chapter 9

1. Pearson, *The Private Lives of Winston Churchill*, 221.

2. Martin Gilbert, *Winston Churchill: The Wilderness Years* (Boston: Houghton Mifflin Company, 1982), 11.

3. Stansky, *Churchill: A Profile*, 52.

4. Ibid.

5. Gilbert, *In Search of Churchill*, 227.

6. Gilbert, *Winston Churchill: The Wilderness Years*, 42.

7. Christian Graf von Krockow, *Churchill: Man of the Century* (London: London House, 2000), 8.

8. Pearson, *The Private Lives of Winston Churchill*.

9. Winston S. Churchill, *Blood, Sweat and Tears* (New York: G. P. Putnam's Sons, 1941), 18.

Chapter 10

NOTE: Churchill's wartime speeches and radio broadcasts are widely available in print and on the Internet. Many of them quoted below are in *Blood, Sweat and Tears*, listed in the bibliography, which is a collection of all his most famous wartime addresses.

1. Churchill, *Blood, Sweat and Tears*, 169.

2. Stansky, *Churchill: A Profile*, 96.

3. Ibid.

4. R. Crosby Kemper III, ed., *Winston Churchill: Resolution, Defiance, Magnanimity, Good Will* (Columbia: University of Missouri Press, 1996), 49.

5. Churchill, *Blood, Sweat and Tears*, 216.

6. Ibid., 219.

7. Paterson, *Winston Churchill: Personal Accounts of the Great Leader at War*, 251.

8. Ibid., 252.

9. Churchill, *Blood, Sweat and Tears*, 297.

10. Ibid., 314.

11. Ibid., 441.
12. Ibid., 462.
13. Lukacs, *Man of the Century*, 182.

CHAPTER 11

1. Phyllis Moir, *I Was Winston Churchill's Private Secretary* (New York: Wilfred Funk, Inc., 1941), 78.
2. Ibid.
3. Ibid.
4. Pearson, *The Private Lives of Winston Churchill*, 24.
5. Ibid.
6. Ibid.
7. Paterson, *Winston Churchill: Personal Accounts of the Great Leader at War*, 28.
8. Churchill, *Never Give In!*, 292.
9. Ibid., 307.
10. Ibid., 312.
11. Ibid., 319.
12. Lukacs, *Man of the Century*, 188.
13. Stansky, *Churchill: A Profile*, 158.
14. Lukacs, *Man of the Century*, 255.
15. Paterson, *Winston Churchill: Personal Accounts of the Great Leader at War*, 290.
16. Lukacs, *Man of the Century*, 269.

CHAPTER 12

1. Lukacs, *Man of the Century*, 273.
2. "The Sinews of Peace," forever known as "the Iron Curtain speech," may be heard at www.americanrhetoric.com. This site also features a complete transcript of the speech, as well as recordings and transcripts of other Churchill speeches.
3. Krockow, *Churchill: Man of the Century*, 282.
4. Churchill, *Never Give In!*, 406.
5. Pearson, *The Private Lives of Winston Churchill*, 339.
6. Krockow, *Churchill: Man of the Century*, 97.
7. Ibid., 286.

8. Kay Halle, ed., *Irrepressible Churchill: A Treasury of Winston Churchill's Wit* (Cleveland: The World Publishing Company, 1966), 345.

9. Ibid.

10. Ibid.

11. Ibid.

12. Roy Howells, *Churchill's Last Years* (New York: David McKay Company, Inc., 1965), 62.

13. Ibid., 153.

14. Ibid.

15. Ibid., 168.

16. Pearson, *Private Lives*, 418.

17. Lukacs, *Man of the Century*, 307.

18. Kemper, *Winston Churchill: Resolution, Defiance, Magnanimity, Good Will*, 198.

BIBLIOGRAPHY

Best, Geoffrey. *Churchill: A Study in Greatness*. London: Hambledon and London, 2001.

Boyle, Peter G., ed. *The Churchill-Eisenhower Correspondence, 1953–1955*. Chapel Hill: The University of North Carolina Press, 1990.

Churchill, Winston S. *Blood, Sweat and Tears*. New York: G. P. Putnam's Sons, 1941.

———. *My Early Life: A Roving Commission*. New York: Charles Scribner's Sons, 1930.

———. *Never Give In! The Best of Winston Churchill's Speeches: Selected by His Grandson*. New York: Hyperion, 2003.

Colville, John. *Winston Churchill and His Inner Circle*. New York: Wyndham Books, 1981.

Gilbert, Martin. *Churchill: A Life*. New York: Henry Holt and Company, 1991.

———. *In Search of Churchill: A Historian's Journey*. New York: John Wiley & Sons, Inc., 1994.

———. *Winston Churchill: The Wilderness Years*. Boston: Houghton Mifflin Company, 1982.

Halle, Kay, ed. *Irrepressible Churchill: A Treasury of Winston Churchill's Wit*. Cleveland: The World Publishing Company, 1966.

Howells, Roy. *Churchill's Last Years*. New York: David McKay Company, Inc., 1965.

Jenkins, Roy. *Churchill: A Biography*. New York: Farrar, Straus and Giroux, 2001.

Keegan, John. *Winston Churchill*. New York: Viking Penguin, 2002.

Kemper, R. Crosby, III, ed. *Winston Churchill: Resolution, Defiance, Magnanimity, Good Will*. Columbia: University of Missouri Press, 1996.

Krockow, Christian Graf von. *Churchill: Man of the Century*. London: London House, 2000.

Lukacs, John. *Churchill: Visonary. Statesman. Historian.* New Haven: Yale University Press, 2002.

_____. *Man of the Century: A Churchill Cavalcade Compiled by Editors of* The Reader's Digest. Boston: Little, Brown and Company, 1965.

Moir, Phyllis. *I Was Winston Churchill's Private Secretary.* New York: Wilfred Funk, Inc., 1941.

Paterson, Michael. *Winston Churchill: Personal Accounts of the Great Leader at War.* Newton Abbot: David and Charles, 2005.

Pearson, John. *The Private Lives of Winston Churchill.* New York: Simon & Schuster, 1991.

Rose, Norman. *Churchill: The Unruly Giant.* New York: The Free Press, 1994.

Ruben, Gretchen. *Forty Ways to Look at Winston Churchill: A Brief Account of a Long Life.* New York: Ballantine Books, 2003.

Sandys, Celia. *The Young Churchill: The Early Years of Winston Churchill.* New York: Dutton, 1994.

Spencer-Churchill. Henrietta, *Blenheim and the Churchill Family: A Personal Portrait.* New York: Rizzoli, 2005.

Stansky, Peter, ed. *Churchill: A Profile.* New York: Hill and Wang, 1973.

ABOUT THE AUTHOR

John Perry has appeared on C-SPAN *Book TV*, *The Janet Parshall Show*, *The G. Gordon Liddy Show*, and other syndicated broadcast shows. He has published biographies of Charles Colson, Gov. Mike Huckabee, Booker T. Washington, George Washington Carver, and Sgt. York.

The CHRISTIAN ENCOUNTERS series

Coming
August
2010

JOHANN
SEBASTIAN
BACH
RICK MARSCHALL

WILLIAM F.
BUCKLEY
JEREMY LOTT

ST. FRANCIS
ROBERT WEST

ANNE
BRADSTREET
D.B. KELLOGG

J.R.R.
TOLKIEN
MARK HORNE

THOMAS NELSON
Since 1798